What they say about

MELISSA MESZAROS

SONG OVER THE BONES

"Weaving between New Mexico and the Pacific Northwest, Melissa confronts heartbreak after a devastating fire, finding solace in the music and D.I.Y. culture of the grunge era. It's always the confessions, through song or story, that connect us with others, and eventually ourselves, and that helps us to heal."
—Gretta Harley, co-founder of Home Alive and co-creator of *These Streets*

"A modern zinger! Movies and music. Romance and love. And when all else fails, more music. You'll enter fully into this American landscape of how we move (literally) through loss and change into the next stage of who we are and want to be."
—Sharman Apt Russell, author of *Standing in the Light: My Life as a Pantheist*

"A brutal and honest look at what it is to be lost and find your way back. In a world of increasing isolation, *Song Over the Bones* is proof that everyone has their own battles to fight, but you aren't alone in fighting them."
—Drew Zucker, artist and co-creator of *Canto* and *The Feeding*

"An achingly beautiful memoir crafted from the ashes, both literal and figurative. Meszaros' preforms a postmortem of a doomed relationship and finds new life in the process."
—E.A. Henson, *Biff Bam Pop!*

OIL ON WATER PRESS
This edition first published in 2025
office@oilonwaterpress.com

SONG OVER THE BONES

Edited by J. BRYAN JONES and VANESSA ANDERSON
Cover design: MARK CRITCHELL < mark.critchell@gmail.com >

10 9 8 7 6 5 4 3 2 1

A CIP catalogue record for this book is available from the British Library

ISBN **978-1-915316-47-9 (paperback)**
ISBN **978-1-915316-48-6 (ebook)**

Oil On Water Press. Original true-life stories and memoir.

Exclusive content at **OILONWATERPRESS.COM**

MELISSA MESZAROS

SONG OVER THE BONES

OIL ON WATER PRESS

DISCLAIMER

THIS BOOK IS a reflection of my personal memories, experiences, and emotional journey. The events, descriptions, and interpretations presented are based on my perspective and may not fully align with the recollections or experiences of others. I have tried to recount these events truthfully, and any resemblance to specific individuals is incidental and unintentional unless explicitly stated.

This work is not intended to defame, malign, or harm any person or entity but to share my own story of growth and resilience.

I'm sick of the pain that I'm feelin', it's weighing me down.
If I could erase it all within just one fuckin' dive.
I wrap you precious around my soul and now I'm letting you go.
As I drown these evil spirits and penetrate the obstacles.

"Seaweed"
Mia Zapata, The Gits

CONTENTS

To all of my friends

PROLOGUE

THERE'S SOMETHING TO be said about *home*. We all grow up differently; an array of experiences created by way of family unit, our parents' lifestyle, actions, financial status, beliefs and religion, location and beyond. These variations in our formative years unfortunately determine our levels of comfort in the future—not only how we view our relationships, but also how we handle them.

I've had many conversations with my siblings about the level of nurture we had as children. How our parents grew up in different times, with their parents living through the depression and post-war era American Dream. My paternal grandfather died when my dad was a teenager; my mother's parents both worked labor and menial jobs well into their sixties to support a family of five. Though we've never discussed it, I believe that my parents grew up struggling to find the same stability and definition of home just as I am; despite being brought up in a brand new craftsman ranch house on a quiet street in the nice—but-not-too-nice—part of town in rural Pennsylvania.

My father often told me, "We raised you to be independent." Nay, a latchkey kid and like many others straddling Gen X-Millennial, left to my own devices. I was distilled in loneliness, mostly without parental guidance, until the very last moment. Both my parents were professionals—my mother was a nurse and my father owned a small business selling tools. They opted to have children later in life, in their thirties, are still together, and retired to a modest home in a community in Florida. My parents and grandparents have had marriages that lasted beyond fifty years.

In the Boomer's eyes, for the sake of posterity in their fight for women's lib, framed by a restrictive social construct, one that continues to shape expectations for women born before and well into Y2K. Not only are we expected to be educated and contribute financially to the household, but we are still somehow expected to meet this Traditionalist Generation criteria: marrying, buying a house, and having children.

I swore that as long as I got one or two of those components, a version of my own family would fall into place. But I struggled with what I wanted because what I learned to be right put me at a constant impasse.

In my twenties, I was impulsive—flighty and fickle.

While everyone pushing thirty settled down, I wanted to be free.

I graduated college when I was twenty-five, got pregnant at twenty-seven, and birthed a stillborn, then proposed to, married and divorced. I hoped to spend the rest of my life with every person I fell for. Thought them to be a secure savior to a fault.

Talk about baggage—feel free to delete me from your palm pilot.

Scarlet letter defective syndrome, but it was just an internal battle between nature and nurture. As if it wasn't bad enough that I shaved my head and listened to rock music, I was a "black sheep". (Though the older I get, the more I notice I inherited my mother's laugh and my dad's bullheaded good sense.)

What I always felt was that I lacked security. Lacked love. Not to say that I've never loved, felt love, or that my parents didn't love me, but there's more value in showing up for my fifth grade talent show performance than buying me a package of yellow Nickelodeon Gak, despite me begging for it.

It probably didn't help that my personal lifetime heroes were radical nonconformists Courtney Love and the late Elizabeth Wurtzel, who, in a 2013 *New York Magazine* article perfectly articulated the chaos of her forties: *"I have no husband, no children, no real estate, no stocks, no bonds, no investments, no 401(k), no CDs, no IRAs, no emergency fund—I don't even have a savings account. It's not that I have not planned for the future; I have not planned for the present."*

It could not be more perfectly said, what living in the moment looks like, this generation, bereft of social net worth or human capital.

Since 2002, I've lived in eight different states, and shared a home with four different significant others, two of which I was married to, the others briefly engaged to; simply to avoid the "why buy the cow" statement. It was still considered normal twenty years ago, still in some small country pockets to a greater number.

In films and sitcoms through the early '90s, characters in their early twenties were still getting engaged and married, as portrayed in televised events like *Saved by the Bell: Wedding in Las Vegas*. No network or sponsor considered the damage this might cause.

All this influence, plus understanding what real love is, is a big ask.

I've learned to forgive myself for a number of decisions, failures, confusion, and have come to a platitude that there might just not be a norm.

When it comes to relationships, I have *no idea* what I'm doing.

This is a story about a distorted version of love, through someone with an insecure attachment style from growing up a latchkey kid, under the influence of the media, compounded by a series of traumas and one big, bad relationship. And when I met *him*—my ex—I was three months into recovery after sustaining a nearly deadly traumatic brain injury (TBI), after being hit by a car in Portland, Oregon. I was suffering from post-concussive symptoms and PTSD. Despite being in therapy, while struggling with such a condition, my decision-making was altered because people in this state are easily influenced and make choices based on emotion rather than logic. I don't excuse the behavior or actions, but where I was in my mind, in recovery, was residual from dissociation; a mental process where a person disconnects from their thoughts, feelings, memories and sense of identity. I had mental regression from trauma after my first dissociative episode.

My ex was the one I'd been waiting for.

His eyes gleamed with such fervor and love that burned a gaping hole right through me.

Picture a school recess wedding, choosing a boy and a fistful of dandelions.

Things moved quickly with us. I had to be his. He had to be mine. He was perfect in every way and if I was to let it go, I'd be waving off my perfect paperback-plotted destiny.

Trauma-based decision-making at its finest.

Eight years later—five since our house caught on fire—this whole chapter wouldn't exist if I knew then what I know now. I wish that I had never met him, found him handsome and perhaps deceptively charming. I was vulnerable in my quest for comfort, for a sense of home, and needing someone to care for me when I couldn't do it alone.

I mean, I'm a city girl—what the hell was I doing living in the middle of the woods with a stranger anyway?

I was a fool for love.

A mess left holding the bag.

The one seeking solace.

Unstable foundations and self-care came all too naturally to me. From this place to that one and one failed relationship to the next—it was burn it to the fucking ground, until it actually did.

What I will give myself is that in this I learned to trust my gut again, and finally ask for and accept help. First as a lark, then a phoenix, through penning what I call a modern feminist tragedy.

This story is about my world being set on fire, of me falling apart.

My aubade to heartache.

The anti-love story.

The self-love story.

A story about *home*.

SIDE A

WHO BY FIRE

YESTERDAY WAS THE anniversary of our house burning down. Today, I got the call from the attorney—it was done. I did a livestream while walking from the liquor store on the east end of Pittsburgh, with a backpack full of Sauvignon Blanc.

"That's it, I guess," I said. "I don't feel any different."

Truth is, at that moment, I didn't—despite all I'd already been through.

The video went live right before I sliced into a whole chocolate cake, clutching a freshly corked bottle while I belted out "The Origin of Love" from the off-broadway musical *Hedwig and the Angry Inch*. The rock opera that begs the question, *do relationships we have with others define us? Have we been unceremoniously split from our other half and need to find them? Will they complete us? Make us whole? Can two people truly become one?*

Had I shown my shorn and shaped self-deprecation on a

whole new level?

No, because a year before, I filmed myself sitting on my bed with mussed-up hair, whining, and another standing at my kitchen table blowing my nose, and then again from a dark hotel room, in a bathtub, drunk and senseless.

Alas, nothing could top my TikTok montage: clips of my ex and I snuggled on the grass at a Parliament Funkadelic show, followed by an emu bursting through the car window during our trip to the drive-thru zoo. The phrase *"No one should end a relationship by ghosting"* positioned dead center, Powfu's "Death Bed" as the soundtrack.

In less than two hours, the post had over four thousand views before I took it down.

I just wanted him to know I was hurting. But he was too wrapped up in his travel vlog, turning my cargo trailer into a home and driving cross-country—avoiding me and all we'd left unresolved. Or maybe he just didn't care.

If I got him with a TikTok, he one-upped me with radio silence.

He wouldn't talk to me.

Recognizing that we ever existed was even too big of an ask.

The trailer he was living in, I purchased because of a U-Haul shortage upon our displacement and relocation from southern Oregon to New Mexico, which I now regret haphazardly joking, "This is where you'll live when you leave me," never once considering he'd actually go off the grid with it.

Nearly two years had come and gone, and lo and behold, my intuition was right.

It was the second week of September. Autumn loomed in my bones. Arms laid out cold. The sunset, too soon. The passing of Labor Day brought this infinite feeling of end.

Where'd summer go?

To relocating. Again.

To the East Coast. Again.

The place I'd call home. Again.

Again—the pattern I hoped to break.

From home to relationships and back and forth in bad habits. A broken-record-dirty-word that I've come to despise as both a verb and in action. Repetition is exhausting. Formulate insanity when expecting a different result, I suppose.

Between my previous marriage and this relationship, I moved into seven different homes—nine since he and I met in July 2018, and a total of twelve homes since 2017—not counting hotels, long weekends, or work trips and vacations.

Oregon, New Mexico, Washington, and back to Pennsylvania. A known nomad in the first half of my life, there was a great desire for permanence as I approached forty. And forty, so it seemed, I'd be facing alone.

So much for the fairy tale ending or Hollywood romance. No *Reality Bites, Singles*—whatever alternative love story is left in my digital library.

It was the idea of love in the movies that led me here in the first place.

The Disney Corporation and its 1989 release, *The Little Mermaid*.

My mother took me out of kindergarten one afternoon to see it. I rarely saw my mom, and I was alone with her at that. This was one of the very few times it wasn't a family affair. Six years old, I don't remember visiting a movie theater before that day, which made it even more magical. The title track of the score against the glimmering animated water, the cavalcade of mermaids wafting above as the credits opened. Glory melted my heart. Not only did I fall in love with the narrative and the black-haired, blue-eyed Prince Eric, but right then and there, I fell in love with *love*. The idea of being in love. Thus began my quest for the perfect storybook version of it.

Could I be part of that world?

Add a soundtrack, a couple more years compounded with even more '90s love stories and their hit songs; consider the blockbusters through the decade *Robinhood: Prince of Thieves* (Bryan Adams, "Everything I Do"), *Titanic*

(Celine Dion, "My Heart Will Go On"), and the ubiquitous and most obvious, *The Bodyguard* (Whitney Houston, "I Will Always Love You"). The way these films and their top-ten hit songs injected this falsified idea of romance felt so visceral and real in the moment as a child watching the world go by in the back seat of my grandparents' four-door Oldsmobile, that I wanted love—*that kind of love*—so much to be true to the point where I considered maybe there was a person somewhere out there, my future person, doing the exact same thing as me at that very moment.

Even without the films, music had (and still has) power. And eventually, I'd find myself sucked into the realms of *High Fidelity,* where the verse-chorus-verse had unprecedented transformational properties. Music, the feeling, and its history and locations, are what helped me keep dreaming and live through it.

That feeling—

One so deep, it's an explosion of endorphins that sends a shiver and shakes down my spine; surging through my arms and fingertips that maximizes to an insatiable brain-gasm.

I'd pick music over a man any day; if the man writes music, aces. Most of them in my life have. I love Kurt Cobain more than I had most of my boyfriends—nothing like being an addict when there's a purveyor that manufactures my drug of choice.

Add a couple of decades and my ex's way with a guitar, and there it was. It all seemed like the perfect ending in my beautiful, severely broken brain. At that time in my recovery, I could barely leave my house, tie a shoe, and couldn't recognize my own face.

"You should avoid making any rash or big decisions at this time," said my therapist.

Which I pooh-poohed because I was wholly convinced there was a tinge of jealousy that I was in a relationship, in love. *If that doesn't exemplify my lacking level of rationale at the time...*

Maybe, most of all, none of this would've happened if the house hadn't burned down in September 2020. The settlement from my brain injury became part of the plan. With the innkeeper holed up in the mother-in-law's quarters behind our rental, privacy was nearly impossible, and buying a house became the goal. For several months, we searched western Oregon with a delightful blonde broker in Columbia hikers. From fixer-uppers with no roof on an apple orchard to a hillside where the elderly owner agreed to throw in a riding mower with a cash purchase.

"I need these high ceilings!" I said, gripping my ex's hand as we marveled at the mid-century modern interior—floor-to-ceiling windows and a sleek open kitchen flowing into a living room centered around a statement fireplace.

I put down the earnest money, along with a promissory note from my attorney, stating that I'd be able to cover the down payment upon receiving the full amount.

But, insurance companies are evil. There was a lien for my medical bills and outstanding attorney's fees. I settled for less than a quarter of what was expected and couldn't afford the house.

Rent-to-own became the option, and with it, we stumbled upon an opulent '70s-style two-story perched on the river—exactly the kind of place my ex could fall in love with. An ivy-draped paradise on one acre of land: a closed garden, dark wooden beams, a wraparound deck, and river access. The downstairs area was perfect for my vintage folding bar with its vinyl-upholstered stools. I couldn't wait to set up the record player, stack my albums, and hang my neon Olympia sign—a beacon of home in this retro dream.

Less than two weeks after moving into the house, the day after Labor Day, a gnarly windstorm blew in. Caused a loose power line to whip off in the middle of the Willamette National Forest, setting everything on fire. No warning because the power and Wi-Fi went out.

I got up at five in the morning. Saw the blaze outside the sliding glass doors.

I scurried through the dark; my ex stood over his phone

trying to figure out what had happened.

The disaster witnessed remains in flashes.

A hellscape.

Emergency vehicles quickly led a caravan of cars to the main safety route.

Spots burning, trees down, buildings and vehicles incinerated.

The orange-red glowing sky in the rearview.

Ambulance and police lights muted by billowing smoke.

More fire blasted through, engulfing homes within moments of fleeing.

Ash flitted down like little gray snowflakes, dusting everything beneath.

We settled into a fail-safe motel thirty miles away to watch the story unfold on the local news, then national news; dots encroached on what was to be our former home, our past and short-lived life near the river.

The motel was the kind of place where time seemed to stop, but not in a charming way. The maroon carpet was worn thin in places, its once-rich color dulled by years of grime and neglect. A scratchy gold comforter covered the bed, its synthetic sheen in the dim glow of the light overhead. The wallpaper, a faded floral print, peeled at the edges and carried a faint mustiness that clung to everything.

I was numb for a moment, knees balled up on the bed. I

stopped, shot him a look, and asked, "You filed for the insurance, *right*?"

He shook his head, which was leaning back on the headboard, and said no. His eyes were fixed on the TV.

I looked over at the hotel desk, at my set of mala beads. Beside them, my coffee tumbler and the little zip pouch I kept my earbuds in; I bought it from Powell's City of Books when I first moved west to Portland, Oregon, in 2006. In the mirror, I noticed the clothes I had on were simply the closest to me when we left: a vintage green *M*A*S*H* T-shirt, a pair of black denim overalls, and an old American Apparel hoodie with the bottom elastic cut off. Doc Martens, a single pair of tube socks, and my ring. I looked like a street punk, a train-hopping oogle, which only added to the irony.

I opened my laptop, pulled out my debit card, and filled out the insurance forms as quickly as possible. I muttered, "We didn't even finish unpacking."

This wasn't the first time we put down roots in the Oregon woodland. It was our second home, nestled in the pines, a place that had once felt like a haven until it, too, became a casualty of chaos.

I never wanted to live in the woods, he did.

I never wanted to leave the city, leave Portland, he did.

Yet you compromise when you love someone.

This was love. My compromise.

Being with my ex meant being in nature.

But at what point does compromise become a sacrifice?

I lament, Disney botched the fairy tale of *The Little Mermaid*. In Hans Christian Andersen's version, written for his queer lover, the mermaid gives up her life to gain a human soul. The witch cut out her tongue so she couldn't speak and split her fin into legs, which were painful to walk upon. Captive, the prince was insistent she danced for him always, just for his amusement, so she did. In the end, the mermaid fails to have him reciprocate her love and she parishes into seafoam.

Whether dissipating into a sea-salted death or trial by fire, love is torment.

CROWN OF THORNS

OLYMPIA, WASHINGTON, FALL 2021. My apartment's all set up, save for a tiny amplifier for my used electric guitar. A cheap futon couch and bed, a cat litter box disguised as an armoire that donned a record player. Beside it, four records: Nirvana, Rodriguez, Broken Water, Superwolf. There was one of each type of flatware, and one plate, one bowl, one pasta dish.

How did I become one again?

Again.

Slowly, slowly.

The APPLAUSE sign he gave me for my thirty-eighth birthday hung over my desk, the last relic of our relationship. It'd been two months since I last saw him. Heard his voice.

Maybe I lived in my head too much. In the '90s too much. But that's how I ended up in Olympia, the real home of "grunge" music—where record label mogul Bruce Pavitt founded Sub Pop as a fanzine in 1980. The home of

K Records, Kill Rock Stars, and the Riot Grrrl movement. Where Kurt Cobain wrote seventy-five percent of his life's work on Pear Street, just a few blocks away from my apartment. I could walk out the front door and turn right to get there, or turn left and end up near his childhood home in Aberdeen, just past Montesano where the band Melvins formed. Add an hour's drive toward Bremerton, and there was the final resting place of Andy Wood, singer of Malfunkshun and Mother Love Bone, and Demri Parrott, the late fiancee of the also late Alice in Chains singer, Layne Staley.

Grunge was, at its core, heavy—a movement for those who challenged adversity and questioned authority. Disaffected, introspective, and cynical. They embraced feminism—from Kurt wearing a dress to L7 championing pro-choice—they celebrated all forms of individuality and weirdness. The grunge aesthetic invited new ways of thinking and broadened horizons.

This music had saved me more than once—first as songs that consoled me in childhood, then as echoes of memories during my recovery. It wrapped around me like a calming plaid cloak, the ultimate form of comfort.

Tacoma in thirty minutes; Seattle, add an hour. South to Portland in two, on a good day. While a former resident of both Pacific Northwest cities, fear kept me from going back to Portland. Seattle's too luxe. But Olympia, "Oly" for short—is a safe, creative space of mine—the halfway mark. A place of refuge and reflection, a place to write—where I churned out countless drafts of my undergrad thesis, my postgraduate work, my first memoir, essays now lost to the ashes of an incinerated external hard drive—even this very book.

There was a need for some form of comfort, familiarity; somewhere so far deep inside my head that nothing else could harm me, and Olympia was it.

My apartment had windows that reached the ceiling and widened to each wall. Through it, an epic view of the Capitol building, the park, and lake below. The ripples in the water hearkened to the stark cold of autumn.

Autumn was ours, he and I, but we wouldn't see our third anniversary together. We celebrated our second despite the wildfire, carving out time to share a seafood platter stuffed in a pineapple.

It was just me, the September issue of *Vogue*, and conveniently, an eviction notice for our rental home back in New Mexico, where we spent our last months together. It wasn't malicious on the landlord's end, more of a savior for me. If I stayed in New Mexico for six months total, by default, my ex would get half of everything without cause.

This spun me out. The anger, the sadness, the confusion.

I'd mastered the art of collapsing wherever and

whenever, since this idea of forever ended.

While our world had already begun to unravel, he committed the ultimate betrayal.

Ghosting is no way to end a relationship.

To boot filing paperwork with an absent partner is difficult, and without a legal residence or documentation—nearly impossible. Between leaving New Mexico for Washington, still with an Oregon ID, and all birth certificates, passports, and social security cards burned and difficult to recover due to the COVID-19 pandemic—it was more than just about jurisdiction. It slowed my process of finding an affordable attorney willing to work with these setbacks.

"We can just hope that he continues his pattern and doesn't respond," the council said. "It'll be a ninety-one-day waiting period, then you'll be you again."

The paperwork was a harrowing nimbus at twenty-some-odd pages. Bank account information, addresses, assets, and belongings, like that stupid Chevy Malibu he left me with, that I'd come to refer to as "Repo Man", if not to inject a bit of cool in the uncool four-door sedan. What was in my possession, what was in his, and what we both left behind in New Mexico.

Along with the documents, I attached pictures of my ex so he could be served.

Wanted Man.

"His hair will most likely be shorter," I said.

I could already hear him scolding me as he was served in front of this girl or that one, a group of strangers, or perhaps on location if he decided to get a job.

Guilt rang out. Guilt for his embarrassment. I questioned if it was all somehow my fault. *Did I give up too soon? Did I not try hard enough?*

"This is where it ends," I said in a winded breath. I looked out the window, the leaves on the trees in the park turning and wilting to a somber brown. "This is it."

It'd been too long since I had seen or heard from him.

Ghosting is a lot like a death you can't reason or reckon with. It's a perilous oeuvre. It's a doom that is unparalleled by any change that no one can surmise.

Gone without reason.

No explanation.

At the time, Erving Goffman's *The Presentation of Self in Everyday Life* was my survival guide, which examines how people perform roles in social settings to shape others' perceptions, likening interaction to a theatrical performance. Amid the heartache and a missing partner, I had to keep up somewhat of a normal, functional routine. Time blurred and all I could do was bury myself in work, which I thankfully did, lucky to be running my publicity firm from home.

Publicity. I was public-facing, always. If anyone could put

on a happy face and put everyone else's needs first, I could. Everyone else, including my ex, got the best of me.

Behind the curtain, I cried while eating Lean Cuisine over the kitchen sink.

It was easier to stay distracted. In your late thirties, there's no room for weakness or fumbling in adulthood. Mastery is expected—anything less feels like failure.

Then I'd pull on my boots and coat and walk to The Brotherhood Lounge, just a few blocks away.

Into happy hour, floating along the planks of Percival Landing, I felt like a deflated Mylar balloon left too long after the party was over. Dangling low, in its sad, pathetic state, where no one has the heart to pop or toss it because of its drugstore price point.

Many of the buildings in downtown Olympia around the bend near Capitol Way were new, with understated oyster restaurants and ice cream, perfect for people passing through.

This is not a place to live unless you can't let go of grunge or simply don't have an agenda for growing up beyond the dreams and liberalism of the '90s. Folks donning thermal underwear and blasting Dinosaur Jr. in storefronts without a hint of irony. Bands and poetry performances spread throughout the area each night, all in the backdrop of personally painted windows, checkered-patterned floors, and come-hither-and-drink-more neon signs. It was a time capsule of defiance, refusing to grow up and reminding anyone who wandered in that some eras never truly end—they just hum along in the background, waiting for someone to notice.

Beyond the West Bay was an incredible view of the Olympic Mountains.

What drew me from the desert to the sea? Crashing waves and soft sand left behind by ebbing tides. Reminiscent of the token of Samuel Taylor Coleridge's "The Rime of the Ancient Mariner" in which a sailor shoots a friendly albatross and is forced to wear its carcass around his neck as punishment.

A twenty from the ATM, through the bellows of red and Christmas-lit vinyl booths, past the projector screen with another muted forgotten black-and-white film.

I tipped back my glass among the fog of cigarette smoke.

One vodka never worked.

Two, not so much.

Three I was wholly convinced I could, so I kept going.

Then four because I had cash left over.

But. I didn't stop.

I was drinking to escape.

All the loss and sacrifice, the time, love, and devotion

that I put into my ill-begotten wreck of a rotten relationship—it was so much easier to blot out than face.

Headphones on, I sulked to Temple of the Dog. Vision spun like a distorted scene in a Dogme 95 film; bulbous droplets of rain on a windowpane, clinging and falling down. Drowned in a sea of sorrow, of sorry, on the salted rim of a margarita. Limp and lambic sloughing through the cold and mile of the inlet, nights often forgotten and easy to forget.

Again on my own, the isolation of a new town, heartache, my age and the digital landscape aren't exactly the most romantic mix when making friends. While some folks partook in polyamory, I found myself amidst barflies dealing with recent breakups and commitment-phobes—even once, a nomadic ayahuasca-brewing silver fox who lived in a Mercedes Sprinter.

He had piercing green eyes, a salt-and-pepper beard, and a chiseled, sun-kissed body that belonged to the wild. We'd wine and dine without restraint, down Aperol, pop Valium to stave off hangovers and let Soundgarden's "The Day I Tried to Live" play on a loop as our spitfire conversations burned through the night.

Only once did he sleep in my bed, and even then, I insisted it stay platonic. He paraded around nude and unbothered, magnetic as ever. In my mind, I wasn't thin or pretty enough for someone so effortlessly untamed. He'd always vanish as quickly as he came, leaving me somewhere between awe and self-doubt.

Romance, no thanks.

Still embarrassed by the whole situation.

Being social meant the backstory unfolding. "My ex ghosted me" isn't easy to say.

They'd recoil, and I wondered what might go through their minds.

What did she do?

Every time I'd expose the truth of a relationship that left me emotionally unhinged, I'd compare myself to others, less damaged, nervous that I didn't measure up because of that smallest slip of phrase with one big red flag. Further, I was on high alert for similar patterns, words, and negative behavior from anyone near me. Manifesting or misinterpreting it, a pointless polarity in the long run. Everyone was a bad guy, everything felt off. I could no longer trust my own decisions because look what happened. All that was left was me—the only person left to blame because he was gone.

This is Complex PTSD. It's like regular PTSD, but with deeper layers—waves of anger or sadness that come out of nowhere, the past bleeding into the present, and a constant wariness that makes trusting feel almost impossible.

So I isolated myself.

A broken shade of self that led to drunk self-indulgence—not thinking twice about stopping myself as the cold rain puttered down.

I slumped on an empty stomach, my heavy head pulled toward the floor.

I looked around, no one was there.

I began heaving.

Water-water everywhere.

Vomit on the floor.

In the restroom.

Darkness.

I woke up next to my toilet, fully clothed.

According to my phone, I texted my college boyfriend.

There was a voicemail from my mom, she sounded worried.

The last time I consumed that much alcohol was in Texas, just that spring. I woke in the shower, cold water beating down, a sodden towel clinging to my torso like a Terry-clothed second skin and another bundled up under my head. I was wearing nothing but a custom bling chain that read "Foie Gras".

The night before, I had one too many mezcal tasters with a group of Michelin chefs from Chihuahua, wandered through an abandoned dirt-floor cabin art installation, and called my best friend Hilary back in Portland to tell her I'd run away—before finally crawling into the shower.

"Wait, wait," she said, her voice buzzing through the phone like static electricity. "You ran away? Like, gone-gone? Where even are you? Are you in Mexico? Are there tequila barrels? Do they even have Wi-Fi?!"

"Hilary, I'm in Marfa, *Texas*."

"*Marfa*?!" she repeated, her voice pitching up like I'd said I was calling from another planet. "Melissa—oh my God, I was just watching *Portals to Hell*! You know, Jack Osborne's paranormal show? They were in Marfa in this episode. Hotel Paisano! Are you staying there? Tell me it's haunted. Is it haunted?"

"No, I'm not at Hotel Paisano. I had to leave the house. It happened again."

"Ohhhh, *himmmmm*," she said, dragging out the word like a bad taste. "What did he do this time? Say something stupid? Or was it one of those *'I'm a tortured soul'* speeches where he turns it all back on you? God, I swear, he's so predictable!"

I sighed. "It's not that simple. I'll explain everything when I get back, okay? I just… I had to go. I couldn't stay anymore."

Her voice softened, but she couldn't help herself. "So, let me guess, he said something dumb, you called him out, and now he's sulking like some wannabe Ram Dass who can't handle basic emotions?"

"*Hilary*!" I said, shaking my head but unable to stop laughing.

"Fine," she said, exhaling. "But seriously, you're okay?"

"I'm okay," I said, smiling back at my broken reflection in the vanity next to the bed.

"Good," she replied. "Because, honestly, he doesn't deserve you. He never did." Her thoughts trailed and quickly derailed. "I wonder if *Ozzy* stayed at the Paisano."

I shook my head. "I'll let you know what I find out."

Her chaotic energy was exactly what I needed, cutting through everything, always. Hilary had a way of making the hardest moments feel ridiculous, and in that ridiculousness, a little bit lighter.

"If you see a ghost, or a rattlesnake, or even anything remotely haunted, you have to call me. Promise me, okay? Like, seriously. Promise!" Then she hung up.

So how'd I get there?

Two days before that, back in New Mexico, an argument broke out with my ex.

We were in my office.

His fists balled.

Forehead protruding.

He raised his voice, and said, "I'm always going to be better than you!"

Chin tucked into his neck. Brows furrowed and beads of

black dilated beneath them. His crooked teeth clenched and his mandible protruded. Gomer Pyle: *Full Metal Jacket*.

He got closer.

I swallowed my breath.

Closer.

I pleaded, "Don't get in my face. Don't get in my face."

"Then shut the fuck up!"

I cinched my eyes and wound my chin tightly into my shoulder.

My body coiled. "Why? Because you can't—"

He stood over me. Towered me. His breathing, indignant.

My eyes opened. Icky thump heartbeat vibrated my shirt.

"Bitch!"

He walked out, slamming the door behind him.

I gasped, exhaled.

I leaped for my phone.

Dialed the National Domestic Violence Hotline.

As I waited, I focused on a wafting tuft of hair on the floor.

"I don't feel safe anymore," I whispered.

The operator asked me to breathe. Be calm. "No one, no matter how they are feeling, should be saying or doing those things to you. Hurt people hurt people."

"It's never been this bad. It's getting worse, I see it. I can't talk about my feelings, that's how this started. I don't know what to do... I'm all alone... He's the only person I know here... Everyone else is thousands of miles away."

"You don't have anywhere to go—can you go to a shelter?" asked the operator.

"My landlord lives on the other side of the fence," I said. "I don't want to get them involved."

"Then call the police."

I hung up. Thinking if anything happened, as long as I made the call, it could be traced.

Waiting until dark, I tiptoed through the back of the house to the bedroom. I shook myself to sleep.

He slept on the couch.

Upon waking, I packed an overnight bag. I had a telehealth therapy appointment that morning; calls I hated taking at home. He would either eavesdrop and comment afterward or yell at me for waking him up by because I was too loud.

He plastered Post-it's all over the bathroom mirror. There was one that read, *"I am not your enemy."*

Hard to believe at that point.

I crept out the front door. It was too early for him to know.

My original plan was to drive to town and take the call, then see how I felt afterward. Aimlessly I walked around the plaza, and my therapist, while I didn't tell her the whole story in detail, encouraged me to take some space.

I stopped at Dennis Hopper's gravesite and contemplated the day among his bandanna-clad cross. Dust circled the tiny graveyard.

Decided to drive south to Santa Fe, but it wasn't far enough.

Santa Fe to Albuquerque, then I'd turn around.

Instead, Albuquerque turned to Las Cruces, and finally, El Paso, to seek out Rosa's Cantina, the famed song from Marty Robbins—just to see if it was real.

I drove nearly four hundred miles through the Southwest, trying to put as much distance as I could between myself and him to erase what happened. But no matter how far I went, I couldn't make sense of it—how somewhere, somehow, a switch in him had flipped. This was not the person I chose. That much, I knew.

Tired, I rented a room in downtown El Paso. On the TV, I caught my silhouette on the plasma screen, faint and ghostlike, staring back.

I texted him: *I'm in El Paso. I'll pay for the wear in the car. I'm sorry, I just couldn't stop. I'm only about two hours from Marfa, so I'm going to drive there tomorrow. I'll be home in a few days.*

I got into the shower, then curled up in bed in a white robe and slippers—sinking into the mattress. Just two weeks earlier, I had done the exact same thing—spent a night in Denver before flying to Florida to see my parents. And two weeks before that, I'd stayed overnight at a spa.

Separating myself had become second nature.

Why?

Time went on and his voice grew louder, words more hurtful, and outbursts closer together. For too long I fought too hard; threw my life away, behest of his wants and needs. At a certain point, escape is needed as a means for sanity, or survival. I was tired of footing the bill, taking care, and shutting up—playing that role. All I knew was that the distance, emotional or physical, was never going to stop expanding unless I stayed quiet. I was tired of rationalizing his behavior. I had little defenses left.

Someone had to take care of me all those nights.

Those blue nights.

Blue nights felt like the world holding its breath—those twilight moments after sunset but before darkness, when a soft haze settled over everything, heavy with melancholy.

Those nights when I was momentarily set free by the music of The Gits—a raw, unapologetic punk band formed at Antioch College in Ohio in the late '80s before they migrated to Seattle as the commercial grunge wave began its rise. Their music wasn't about polished hooks or hits—it was an open wound, raw energy that stood in stark contrast to the radio-friendly chart-toppers they were billed alongside. The scene itself often overshadowed The Gits, who lived among it but remained distinctly punk.

Their singer, Mia Zapata, was a poet who reigned as a charismatic punk rock Bessie Smith—she penned and belted lyrics that deeply resonated in my soul. Songs like "It All Dies Anyway", "Sign of the Crab", and the incomparable single "Second Skin", ring out with such annihilating fervor and gusto that it's impossible to ignore that level of audial penetration that takes over. Mia sang from the depths, a place that most can never reach—she sang about heartache, drinking, and displacement with palpable passion. Her vocals and her songs, both furious and haunting, echoed the parts of me that I didn't have the courage to voice. A fleeting respite, where the world cracked open for a brief moment, just long enough to remind me I was still breathing.

It's heartbreaking that when people talk about The Gits—or Mia Zapata—her death is often the first thing that comes to mind. In 1993, she was found in Seattle's Central District, raped and strangled with the strings of her hoodie, her life stolen just blocks from where she'd last been alive—leaving The Comet Tavern late one night. Friends and bands pulled together to organize raising money for a private investigator, only to track down the perpetrator, a complete stranger, ten years later. Her cold case was the first to be solved in the state of Washington by saliva DNA evidence. Her killer was indicted, tried, and thrown in prison. He died in January 2021. To me, Mia Zapata's tragic death is merely a footnote to her immense talent. Death may have made Mia an icon, but her poetry is what makes her human—a stark reminder that not everyone makes it out alive.

GODDAMN LONELY LOVE

NEW MEXICO, SPRING 2021. Caesar salads and burgers coated in hatch green chile were on every menu. The ladies, who lunched in their plasticine faces, sipped pinot, shuffled through bags worth thousands, and waited for their husbands to call and inform them of the arrival of their private jets. The rest of the retirees remained holed up in small, gentrified pockets, weaving looms or cultivating goji berries as if their day-to-day hippie actions were a virtuous gift to the world.

Moving to where there was more dirt than trees, away from Oregon, was the agreement. We rented an old adobe house in a small village with a burn area plagued with scorched stump shards stuck in the ground; I wanted to live in Santa Fe. Luckily, there was 5G, and the house was mostly furnished. Never in all my years of moving from the East to the West Coast did I ever picture myself relocating so far south to live on such desolate land. Life had been hollowed out, so it seemed a good fit.

The donkeys and llamas on the property were cared for by the landlord, the only child of a renowned New York filmmaker from the cultural decade. They lived in a modest house next door and spun Mongolian goat hair on a spindle.

Set at the gorge where the Rio Grande meets Colorado, spring melted into desert sunrises and monsoon evenings brought on by the high elevation. The sky was an endless opus, with rain tracing patterns far off in the distance. Forked lightning moved upward, illuminating the vast, empty wall of my office.

My ex left his job without the prospect of work upon relocation, to focus on finding a life's passion, leaving me as the breadwinner. I was tethered to a desk all but one day a week to make ends meet.

"The woman I bought a treadmill from is starting a business and offered a free somatic facial," I told him one Saturday afternoon. "Not sure what that means."

He nodded and went back to scrolling his phone.

I threw on some clothes, tied my hair back, and stepped into my Chucks.

The Bluetooth cut in and out until just past the historic district, where the murals and adobe buildings were adorned with Kokopelli—the God of Harvest and Plenty—who was thought to bring growth and joy.

Driving was the only way to smudge out my feelings of isolation. I wondered if it was a form of conditioning—an adaptation from living so far away from everything and everyone for so long. It felt as though my lockdown had begun long before the rest of the world's, spurred by the head injury that confined me to a private kind of quarantine. For much of my recovery, the outside world was a source of anxiety—overwhelming in its brightness, its noise, its sheer presence. Light sensitivity and overstimulation made even the simplest acts, like stepping outside, feel like an insurmountable challenge. Isolation wasn't just a state of being; it became a lens through which I viewed recovery—a simultaneous retreat and reckoning with what it meant to exist beyond what knocked around in my mind.

I pulled into the parking lot next to four small connected orange buildings. A short-haired brunette stood outside, cradling two tiny pugs in her arms. She gently caged them before gesturing me inside her makeshift spa. Though it was daytime, the pastel pink room was dimly lit by flickering candles, casting soft shadows on the walls. A massage table dominated the center of the room, flanked by two chairs. Behind a pair of long white curtains, I caught a glimpse of a desk tucked away, adding a hint of mystery to the intimate space.

She motioned for me to sit, then handed me a stack of

Tarot cards to shuffle. "What is your intention for this session?" she asked, her voice calm but pointed.

I crossed my legs at the ankle. "I thought this was a facial?"

Her lips curved into a faint smile. "The cards help me focus on areas of tension relief," she replied. "What's your focus? Work? Relationships? Personal goals?"

Still uncertain, I plucked a few cards from the stack and laid them on the small table between us, the air thick with unspoken curiosity.

"The cards will let me know," she said, her gaze intent as she reached for the spread. Her fingers, thin and delicate like birthday candles, hovered briefly before flipping each one over with purpose.

The first card, The Suit of Cups: Consciousness associated with love and relationships.

The second, Two of Swords: Decisions, at an impasse, avoidance.

Third, The Tower: Chaos, revelation, awakening.

Her eyes softened, and she shifted her gaze to me. "Is your relationship causing you stress?" she asked, moving her fingertip to touch the next card. "Because you should avoid any personal doubt—it's headed toward destruction."

The idea of anyone questioning my love and dedication was a first, and frankly, I was offended. "We moved here because we lost our house in a wildfire," I said. "So you're wrong."

She put up her palms in soft defense.

I continued, "Thanks, but I think I'm good on the whole *facial thing*—I should go."

I fumbled for my car keys and stood up. The space felt even smaller, with barely enough room to maneuver between me and the door.

I started up the car to head home, wondering if I should've stopped anywhere on the way. There was a jewelry store. Then I thought to stop for a burger, maybe coffee. Simple things I could do alone. He was never one for leaving the house or going out, so I had grown used to filling the gaps myself, to the point where it barely fazed me anymore.

Dusk was quickly approaching, so each idea fell away as I moved closer to home. I cranked "Seven Angels" by the band Earth, and lost myself among the sagebrush and humps of hills in the far-off distance. Descansos, or crosses on the side of the road left to remind people of the dangers of travel, lined the shoulder.

A gray apparition in my periphery darted across the front of my car. I pumped the brakes and swerved to the right, pausing to catch my breath, my heart racing.

What the fuck!?

It was the biggest dog I'd ever seen.

What the fuck.

I quickly surveyed the land. The desert.

It was a Mexican wolf.

Shook, I texted Hilary: *A wolf just ran in front of my car.*

She called immediately and shouted, "OH MY GOD! That's your SPIRIT ANIMAL!"

I laughed, the adrenaline still coursing. "More like an illusion from lack of oxygen."

Something was contributing to my general malaise because since we arrived in New Mexico, I just felt off. The desert has scarce resources, and the excessive heat and extreme cold make it hard to survive. Amazing how opulence could make for such claustrophobia. For as vast as the desert was, there was no room to breathe, and elevation sickness was pretty common for the beachcombers vacationing at the local ski resorts. It was a divisive way to sell cans of H2O, which reminded me too much of whippets to take seriously.

Instead of fresh air, there were oxygen bars and oxygen therapy—rebranded as "fusion healing practices" in bourgeois apothecaries—nestled conveniently beneath gluten-free, vegan, sustainably sourced restaurants.

On a whim, I booked an appointment: *Heal and alchemize pain, acknowledge numbness, and access your vision of the future.*

The host offered me tea and requested that I wait quietly for the Shaman. "Don't release any energy," they warned.

Come for the oxygen, stay for the woo-woo.

The waiting room had the ambiance of a college dorm, with beads and tapestries strewn about. The Shaman emerged from the stairwell into the dimly lit foyer, a drum cradled in their hands. With a practiced motion, they swung a long braid behind their back, their movements deliberate and calm. Their voice was steady, almost melodic, as they invited me into the meditative space.

"Do any smells bother you?" they asked. "Any sounds?"

I didn't have the patience to explain that my sense of smell was nearly nonexistent, so I joked, "Sounds? You have a high-pitched valley girl stashed in that closet?"

Their expression didn't waver, entirely unamused. "Lay down and close your eyes with your hands at your sides."

They placed the oxygen tube over my head and in my nose.

The lights dimmed through the skin of my eyelids.

The drum started.

The Shaman began chanting words I couldn't make out in my half-slumber.

Somewhere between trying to discern whether something was on me or hovering over me, amid the dizzying haze of an oxygen high, an hour slipped by unnoticed.

I opened my eyes to find the Shaman removing crystals from my body.

They were quiet for a moment, then abruptly said, "You're not listening to the wolves."

I went to sit up.

The Shaman placed their hands on my shoulders.

"For serious?" I lay there, awestruck. *I didn't mention the fucking wolf.*

"The wolf spirit brings instinct, wisdom, and an appetite for freedom. The Wolf Woman, or *La Loba,* collects the bones of those creatures in danger of getting lost."

My eyes warmed, then watered.

They continued, "We start as a bundle of bones and it's our job to recover them. When these bones are assembled and sung to, the soul is resurrected as our true self."

There were too many coincidences to ignore in too short of a period, each one stacking like a signpost pointing me in a new and unknown direction.

That night, I stayed at the El Rey Court.

White sconces. White Adobe walls. Everything minimalist white.

On the patio at La Reina, the hotel bar, an open cover had vines that swayed gently.

I opened my journal and wrote:

Last night I had a dream that punk icon Keith Morris kissed me on the forehead and told me I was pretty. I drove to Santa Fe and purchased a shawl from the Saturday Farmer's Market. Outside one of the high-end stores, admiring a pair of Golden Goose sneakers in the window, I caught a glimpse of a handsome older man with a septum ring looking and smiling in my direction. I wish my partner would look at me the way that man did. Instead, he's going down that dark road again. I crave a man's touch. Every single man—old bikers to well-dressed fellas and guys driving lowriders—it all looks good when you're lonely. I've tried to get my partner to notice me, but he declines my advances. I never knew you could feel so alone while with someone.

Dropping my pen, I swirled my drink with two black stirs, the melting ice fusing with proof and lime. I'd never felt so far from home, so far from a breath, so dead from life. Corroded metal, frayed rope and wood. Everything around me showed wear.

The sky was gray, releasing thick raindrops that splashed against the pavement. Steam rose from the puddles, curling and shifting, carried by the wind in hypnotic waves. Each ripple danced in unison, rising and falling with every gust, yet somehow existing apart, each drop a solitary rhythm in the storm's symphony.

HELLO IT'S ME

HE ENDED IT on a neon pink Post-it note scrawled in black pen: *"I miss you already. Thank you for everything."*

In *Sex and the City,* Jack Berger broke up with Carrie Bradshaw on a post-it. But Jack is fictional, so is Carrie. It goes without mentioning that the infamously virile and endlessly sexy "Mr. Big" is fictional as well. Big was Carrie's on-again, off-again emotionally avoidant love interest who eventually became her husband.

When winter came, *And Just Like That...* the new chapter of *Sex and the City*, aired on HBO Max, I witnessed Mr. Big keel over from a heart attack after a ride on his Peloton.

Any last semblance of love I had, died with Mr. Big.

In my black SJP tutu dress, holding a cosmopolitan poured from a pre-mixed bottle purchased at Target, I begged... screamed in horror, *"NO! NO! NO!"* as the exceptional performance of the 3-2-1 countdown of Big's heart slowed, then stopped, as he slumped toward Carrie, who held him close.

But, it gets worse.

Within days, actor Chris Noth, who played the dreamboat tycoon character since 1998, was accused of sexual assault. His career plummeted, Peloton stocks crashed. I marveled at the magnificent collapse of pillars. Fans everywhere were pissed, and it showed.

I guess sometimes it's difficult to separate the art from the artist.

But the character, Mr. Big, was an asshole.

For six painstaking seasons, plus two films, the compulsively aloof New York investment banker tugged and pushed and pulled his girlfriend Carrie in every other which way to avoid commitment, yet we all *still* loved him. Even in the final season of *Sex and the City*, after she told him to fuck right off forever, he followed her to Paris, and in that one cliched romantic gesture allowed not just Carrie, but all the frothing fans, to cheer them on as they confirmed a happily ever after.

Ten years later, he stood her up at the altar and she *still* took him back; we all cheered again when they tied the knot.

All for Mr. Big to die in Carrie's arms? Bullshit.

Enter Carrie's shrill long lost confidant, Susan Sharon, who, at Mr. Big's funeral, noted how much of a prick he was. *Bravo!*

Carrie got this, and I got a note.

And then, two days later, my ex posted to his Instagram that he was in Amarillo, Texas.

I was closing tabs on my laptop, which he sometimes used. He'd left his email open.

TITLE: eHarmony: You have a new message.

I sat up. *What?*

Kneejerk, I opened the email and clicked the profile.

For weeks, he'd been talking to a young Christian dental hygienist from Wisconsin—brown bob and all teeth.

What the actual fuck.

I scrolled through their chat.

He wrote: *I love your housewife vibe... my girl will be home soon... I'm protecting her feelings... talking to you today brought a smile to my face.*

My eyes blurred, my heart burned, my hands trembled.

But I—

Just.

Kept.

Reading.

Paragraph after paragraph, immersed in their dialogue. I'd been discarded. Still paying the bills; while he still slept in our bed and ate meals I prepared.

I called him, no answer.

Then I called Mika in Seattle, a college friend I'd been

sharing screenshots with.

"Do you believe this shit?" I said, pacing back and forth in the living room.

"Did you try to call him?" she asked.

"Yes," I said, frustration lacing my voice. "Straight to voicemail."

She didn't hesitate. "You need to leave. Immediately."

I paused, glancing back at the eHarmony exchange still open on my screen. "I deal with this," I said, my voice cracking. "I love him, and I don't know why. This is all so fucked."

"Melissa, I'm coming down there," she said firmly. "You shouldn't be alone."

"I think I'm going to drive to Albuquerque this weekend," I blurted out, barely hearing her. "I just can't be here—"

She cut me off. "Let me come out there. I'll spend a couple of days with you. We can talk about this. I'll fly down on Thursday."

It was a chance at rescue, but I wasn't sure I had the courage to take it. It was Sunday. The days in between left me contemplating a dark spiral, dreading I'd sit with these thoughts for too long.

In the desert, the ocean of sky goes for miles, into infinity, into the lostness which I felt beyond existence. That night, from my lawn chair on the back porch, I watched the lights flash in the rifted sky—fraught in a past and present and future that felt so dissonant, it presented itself in a phosphine capacity. Darkness, wombs of clouds. A wary, discernible instability that I was all too familiar with to walk away from.

Thunder bellowed. I hurried to take down the metal-framed canopy, my hands fumbling against the rising wind, just in time for the rain to come down.

I wandered aimlessly through the old house, moving from the couch to the kitchen, upstairs to the bed, and back again—circling round and round, grasping for any sense of grounding.

Days passed without a word from him.

Each time I called, it went straight to voicemail, the unanswered ring cutting deeper each time.

I'd sit slumped in a lawn chair, its legs uneven on the concrete slab smattered with chicken poop, and stared off into the distance. A cold Topo Chico nestled between my chest and overalls. The world around me was quiet, save for the occasional rustle of weeds.

I thought about the trips we took to the Oregon coast—nights by the fire pit where the warmth wrapped around us like a promise. I'd haphazardly attempt old cheerleading dance routines from high school, my legs kicking too high, arms flailing out of sync. Those moments felt untouchable, effortless.

How did it get here?

In the days before he vanished, things felt off—like he was hiding something. He went to the mini-mart to buy a pack of cigarettes. He was gone for two hours. When he returned, he said he had run into some TikTok vanners, then shared a six-pack of beer in the parking lot with another gentleman passing through.

A few nights before that, he went into town for dinner alone and said he'd met a group of construction workers who took to him.

I never knew him to be social, let alone spend money frivolously on dining out, especially because I was always the one picking up the check.

I called Hilary. "Still can't reach him."

Her voice stammered before lifting, hesitant. "Do you remember when you went to Florida to visit your parents? Well... he was trying to FaceTime me... a lot."

"Really?"

"Yeah," she said cautiously, "He would call me, ask me to watch movies with him. I always thought of him like a brother or... friendish, your dude... until this one time he was drunk, flipped the camera and, well, I saw his... you know." Her voice dipped, uneasy. "It wasn't an accident. It was... weird."

I sighed, the air growing heavier.

She pressed on, "I never put two and two together. He just kept saying he was lonely and needed someone to talk to."

"He could've talked to me," I replied, my tone sharp with frustration. "He never tried, even when I asked if he was okay."

"Dude, we're best friends. Seems like triangulation to me," she said bluntly. "Like when people bring a third person into a relationship to shake shit up."

I paused, the realization dawning with a painful clarity. "My god, he actually made me angry with you! He said you were texting him all the time, and I know you're a sporadic texter. I was sitting there wondering why you were texting him and not me, but now it makes total sense."

The heaviness of it all settled between us, the silence speaking volumes.

The anger shot up within me. Fuck with me, but don't you dare fuck with my friends.

I texted him: *I know about eHarmony. You need to come home.*

In the passing hours, nothing happened. Darkness remained darkness, and night stretched on as night. I lay in bed, caught in the unquiet endlessness. Nothing but a higher-than-heaven moon hovering beyond the window. Shock and starkness sunk so low. I could tell no difference between my body and the bed frame and the floor or the ground beneath it. I waited for the day, no sleep would come. I turned on the record player in hopes of finding morning.

Eternal Sunshine of the Spotless Mind.

Are you here, are you there, are you fucking anywhere?

It was still too early, and I'd been awake far too long.

Walking into the dining room, I reached for my scissors, then my hair.

I grabbed my car keys.

Out the gate.

Let the road be the only home I know.

The latchkey kid set out in search of comfort, of somewhere, of something—just as I had when I was young, to this friend's house or that one, circling my bike round and round the block just so I had momentum.

Momentum to fill the void.

In the three-hour drive to Albuquerque, I tried my hand at pronouncing the names of pueblos canvassed across each bypass, looping "At The Hop" by Devendra Banhart on my stereo.

I stopped for yellow frilly underwear from Madewell and baggy jeans from Lucky before checking in at the El Vado Motel.

Halfway hipster, the baby blue and eggshell-colored motif featured a swimming pool and an open bar—charming touches that hardly compensated for the wedding party that had usurped the patio. I stepped out of my room in a black corset bodysuit and my freshly coiffed platinum bob. I didn't give a fuck.

Moments later, I hopped into a Lyft and headed downtown, the city lights streaking across the window as I watched the streets shift. At the end of the main drag, a venue ahead buzzed faintly. It was the kind of place where sound bled into the sidewalk.

Albuquerque is a mnemonic of the early 2000s, a lethal sickening injection of Paris Hilton saying *"That's hot"* with unwelcomed stabs of Nu metal in between. Everyone around me faceless, nameless, and unmentionable through the plumes of smoke rolling inward from the street. For as many bars and dives I'd sauntered into across time, it was hardly magnetic; pathetic rather. They played Tad's *Inhaler* album between sets, its raw, heavy riffs, and deep vocals pulling me back.

Homesick.

When I was a teenager, I'd flip on Nirvana's *In Utero* and let the rawness of it carry me away, dreaming of the wonderment of the Pacific Northwest. Wrapped in a blanket, eating saltines, I'd sit on the front porch as the rain fell, imagining a life far beyond the horizon. In my dreams, all I'd own was a bed with a wrought iron frame and a couple of guitars—nothing else seemed necessary. It wasn't about having things; it was about being somewhere that felt like it truly belonged to me.

More than Seattle, I missed Portland—the place that had shaped me. It was where I attended undergrad, was shepherded into the local music scene, and spent nearly fifteen years cultivating myself—my entire adult life up to that point.

I love Portland for its small-town feel, accessibility, unapologetic weirdness, amazing food, and love of books. It was a haven where publishing thrived, guest lists were easy to come by, and it was perfectly normal to read at a bar. With its bagpiping Darth Vader, Voodoo Donuts, airport emotional support alpacas, and feminist strip clubs—Portland was proudly and beautifully strange.

I missed it.

I missed my friends.

My old life.

I hung my head, feeling that I faded into nothing. "Seriously, fuck this."

Over my shoulder, a lanky man in a sagging black T-shirt with long red hair lit a cigarette. He leaned in, the faint smell of smoke curling around us, and asked, "You alright?"

"No. I'm not. Thanks."

"There's an open seat at our table if you'd like. We don't bite."

I shrugged, following him over, more out of politeness.
We ordered a round, I faked a smile.
All I could think was: *he's not coming back*.

OPERATOR (THAT'S NOT THE WAY IT FEELS)

MIKA SET UP her workstation at the kitchen table, cords sprawled, snaking to every outlet. Her head darted between two glowing screens. Outside, a donkey's bray ripped through the valley.

I impatiently watched the stream of coffee fill the carafe. "I'm glad you're here," I said, my voice clipped. "I can't stay. I think I need to leave."

Mika didn't even pause, her fingers still clacking away at the keyboard. "Okay. I'll cancel my flight. We'll drive back to Seattle."

"Can I stay with you, just until he comes back?" I asked, pouring coffee into my cup.

She stopped, turned.

That look.

Sharp. Knowing.

I let out a breath. "You're right. He's not coming back." My words, stagnant. I sat down at the table, and my gray tabby climbed onto my lap. "But what do I do with all this stuff? It's *our* stuff."

I scanned the room: an abalone shell on the windowsill, his guitar case slouched in the corner, the ring he left behind like it had been waiting for me to find it. My cheeks puffed; lips blew a raspberry. "Fuck it. We'll pack light. Pets, the important stuff. Everything else can stay."

Mika smirked, barely. "Light's good."

We packed fast.

Clothes shoved into bags, suitcases.

My cats watched, tails twitching—my tiny dog wide-eyed, circling my feet. Three checks taped to the door for the landlord, no note, no explanation.

I quickly texted him: *Left you rent. You can have everything.*

Mika tried to slam the trunk shut. "Shit," she muttered, giving it one last shove. When it finally clicked, we both laughed, short and sharp. "Road trip!" She threw her hands in the air.

The house shrank, then the village, then the pueblo—collapsing behind us like a bad memory.

I didn't look back.

What was there to miss? Memories I didn't want.

The road ahead, empty and endless. Mika fiddled with

her phone—recording the drawn out nothing of the desert plains.

I looked at her and said, "You know this shit goes on forever, right?"

She laughed.

By the time we reached Arizona, the tall pines from the higher elevations thinned out, shrinking into scraggly, windswept bushes. The air got hotter, thicker, as the elevation sank and rose, the mountains rolling on. Mika pressed her face to the window as we dipped into valleys. "It's like the trees are running from us," she muttered.

"They know better," I said, gripping the wheel tighter.

The desert, vast and pale, was an ocean of dust. When we pulled into a gas station outside Beatty, Nevada, the sunlight bounced off the asphalt harshly. Mika grabbed a water bottle while I filled the tank.

"Look at *that*," she said, pointing across the lot. A sign for the Alien Cathouse Brothel blinked neon."That is *too good*," she said, already heading inside.

The gift shop smelled of bad perfume and regret. Mika grabbed a baseball cap scrawled in green letters. "Matching ones?" she asked, tossing one at me.

"Obviously," I said.

Back on the road, Mika turned to me, dead serious. "We peaked back there. Now it's all downhill."

We rented a shoddy two-star room in Las Vegas with outdoor entry to avoid sneaking the pets through the lobby. Our hotel window overlooked the chaos, the glowing casinos cast reflections onto the walls like some surreal, otherworldly painting. The lights blurred in a relentless pulse—bulbs of red, blue, and yellow flickering off the glass and black asphalt. They drowned out the stars, turning the night restless and electric.

Mika looked out the blinds. " Kind of reminds me of Taiwan," she muttered before shutting them.

The next morning, as we drove toward Reno, she squinted at the horizon. "Why's the sky brown?"

"Fuck if I know—Nevada's gross?"

It was smoke from the Tahoe fires choking the landscape.

Mika cracked the window, then gagged and rolled it back up. "It smells like someone's burning... everything," she said.

I didn't reply, just kept driving into the haze.

Tonopah sprawled under the brutal desert sun, weathered buildings slouching into the dirt like they were too tired to stand. Faded motel signs leaned crookedly, their peeling paint blending into the dust that seemed to swallow the town whole.

My phone buzzed.

His name lit up the screen.

My heart torqued tight.

Suddenly, The Clown Motel jutted out against the flat expanse of the desert like a neon fever dream, its marquee plastered with cartoonish faces, their grins too wide, too frozen, too wrong. My hands turned the wheel, and before I knew it, I slammed on the brakes, skidding into the lot. The tires screeched, kicking up a cloud of dust around us. I yelled at the top of my lungs, "CLOWN MOTEL!"

Mika flung a hand against the dash, eyes wide. "Jesus Christ!"

Now parked, I jabbed a finger toward the motel. "The Clown Motel, it's like, world-famous!" I was already fumbling for my phone with my free hand. "It's creepy. Haunted. People love this shit."

It was the perfect distraction.

I wasn't ready to snap back to reality.

Mika squinted at the sign, her face morphing into something between disgust and amusement.

"I mean, look at it!" I said, kicking the car door open. I stepped out, the heat pressing down on my scalp. I snapped a few photos of the grotesque pastel sign.

Mika stayed in the car, her hat tilted down to block the glare.

When I slid back into the driver's seat, she shook her head.

I started the car and cranked up the radio before any

thought could take hold.

Bruce Springsteen's "Hungry Heart" blasted through the speakers.

We continued on, the sky growing heavier from the Tahoe fires, turning the horizon into a muted smear of orange and gray.

Mika leaned her head against the window. She didn't say a word, and I wasn't about to break the silence. It wasn't uncomfortable, though—it was the kind of silence you slip into with someone who knows when you need it.

Reno appeared suddenly. The streets felt different, tighter, like they were leaning in too close. We found a place called Death & Taxes, tucked into the edge of the city with its sleek black facade and dark, inviting atmosphere. It had a speakeasy vibe, the kind of place that made you forget the outside world existed.

I ordered the most expensive drink on the menu—a Baller Sazerac that came in a tiny, Nick and Nora glass. It radiated arrogance and stunk of licorice. I took a sip, wincing and gagging as the burn hit hard and fast, while Mika stared at me from across the table.

"Give me that!" she said, snatching it from my hand. She took a small sip, her whole face contorting. *"Fuck. Eww."*

"Right?!"

Mika grabbed her thermos, poured the rest of the Sazerac into it with a quick, practiced motion, and screwed the lid on tight. "We're not wasting this," she said. "You don't spend that much on a drink just to leave it."

I shook my head, smiling. "You're amazing."

Leave it to Mika—saving my ridiculous drink like it was some noble act of frugality and defiance.

I let out the first real laugh I'd managed in a long time, then shook my head. "This is why I keep you around."

"Damn straight!" she said, stuffing the thermos in her bag.

The drive to the airport felt shorter than it should have.

I held off on reading his text the entire way, the screen burning in my pocket, waiting for the right moment to tell her. As we pulled into the drop-off lane, I finally opened it. The words stared back at me, mocking, biting.

I looked at Mika. "He doesn't appreciate me making such GRANDIOSE decisions without him," I said, flat and bitter, the sarcasm thick in my voice.

Mika raised an eyebrow, her expression deadpan. "He should've thought of *that* before he logged onto eHarmony."

She pulled her bag from the trunk, slinging it over her shoulder. "Be careful driving," she said, as if reminding me that I'd be the only one who could mess up a straight shot.

I turned the ignition and quickly rolled down the window to catch her before she could disappear inside. I called to her, "Hey, Mika—I think I want to live in Olympia."

She stopped, gave a quick thumbs up, and continued toward the terminal.

I drove off.

Alone in the car, I stared out at the landscape, warped and ghostly.

The horizon with its jagged curves of the Sierra Mountain Range were too bent and broken to imagine what lay beyond it.

I-5 North by way of Sacramento, felt endless—barren fields, dead trees, fields tinting everything sallow. The highway didn't change until I reached Mount Shasta—twisty and charred, it was only the remains of a once-fecund paradise.

There was a huge part of me that blotted out the fire, the days after, and those leading up to the realization that everything we had was gone.

In the face of an air advisory, I insisted on sitting out under the lamppost of the temp home we were placed in—one creepily without a television, too many children's toys, and framed photos of the owner's travels abroad. At least if I sat outside and inhaled toxins, I'd get a lot closer to how I already felt inside.

Never mind the hero—

If I had not woken up that morning—

Never mind that Mika organized a crowdfund, supported by so many amazing people to whom I was deeply grateful—

Never mind that I had the animals, and at the time, him, though emotionally a million miles away—

Never mind. *Oh well, whatever.*

Amy Winehouse crooned softly as I arrived in south Oregon, where life with my ex had begun. The sky turned overcast.

I stopped for a vanilla cone with rainbow sprinkles, gave water to the cats and dog, and continued on to stay the night with my friend Masie in Eugene.

Masie was a free spirit, she insisted on honing witches' powers and followed the Tarot while foraging for magic mushrooms. We met while she was working as a bank teller, but after a palm reading, decided to leave her job to open a Wiccan shop.

She took me out for pizza the same day my ex gifted me the *APPLAUSE* sign.

When I got home that evening, he was slumped on the couch, watching music videos. The sharp angles of his face caught in the TV's glow, his glasses reflecting the screen like a shield. His red cap was tilted low, as if to block out anything else he didn't want to see, but his glassy eyes darted toward me the moment I walked in. The faint scent of alcohol lingered in the air, and his scruffy beard, meant to look careless, only added to his overall disheveled edge. He seemed annoyed that I'd stayed out, though I could never be sure. His stonewalling was always calculated—bait for a fight I wasn't going to take.

On the screen, Limp Bizkit's "Break Stuff" blared.

"Ugh, *Limp Bizkit*," I said. I hate Limp Bizkit.

His head snapped toward me, and his eyes narrowed, hard and cold. Without warning, the yelling started—*fuck this, fuck that, fuck you*—words I'd heard so often, I wished they'd lost their sting. His voice carried the kind of condescension that always made me feel smaller, like he could shrink me down with volume alone.

I turned and started walking away. He hated that more than anything, but I'd learned from Paul Colaianni's *Love and Abuse* podcast that disengaging was my only recourse.

"If you're going to continue to be this way, I'm done. This is stupid," I said calmly, not even turning back. I walked straight into the bathroom, shutting the door behind me to wash my face.

His yelling continued, muffled, but his tone shifted—dropped into something quieter, more sinister. I heard him murmur, "I don't feel safe... send someone."

I froze, the faucet still running. I gasped.

He didn't feel safe?

Projection is the funhouse mirror of emotional abuse.

They take their own baggage, their ugly little truths, and hurl them at you as if they were yours.

It wasn't about me—it was never about me—but I was always to blame.

Talking to him was like tiptoeing through a minefield.

Even a harmless comment could set off an explosion.

That was my first mistake.

We'd only just settled into a home after months of being uprooted, but it felt like there wasn't enough room for both of us. The emotions in the apartment were too charged. He didn't seem to like living in the city—or, more likely, that I thrived there. I moved freely, made friends, found things to do without him. I was regaining control of my brain, myself, my surroundings. He was losing his grip.

I stepped out of the bathroom, blotting my face with a green terry towel, my heart racing. I hesitated, then asked, "Did you just call the police?"

His expression didn't change, his face flat and unreadable. "I didn't."

"Then *you pretended* to call the police?"

His glassy eyes darkened, his jaw tightening. "Are you crazy?"

I steadied my voice. "You started yelling. We have a difference of opinion. That's all it is. You raised your voice, then I guess pretended to call the police—I would never do that to you. I would never—"

"Are you crazy... are you crazy... *are you crazy*?" His voice rose, mocking, each repetition sharper than the last.

"You're drunk," I said softly, trying to defuse him.

He stammered, "What have I drank?! I don't even have a cup!" He gestured wildly at the room, his movements exaggerated, his voice dripping with defensive anger.

I softened my tone further, forcing calm into the chaos. "I just want to know why you would pretend to call the police."

He stared at me, his expression deadpan, his voice colder than ever before. "Because I wanted to scare *the shit out of you*."

He didn't need to yell this time. His actions and words were so calculated, precise—designed to cut—and they did.

This stayed with me, heavy and suffocating, until I found myself in Masie's backyard, spilling the details of every argument with my ex in their entirety. The weight of knowing most of the truth but not all of it, waiting for the gaps to be filled.

I sat cross-legged on a metal chair, surrounded by the cigarette dregs left by the other tenants and a stray cat named Bruce.

Masie didn't press me further.

She didn't need to.

She just sat there, her steady presence cracking open the space between us.

When she leaned in to hug me, the soft scent of palo santo clung to my cheek.

I came up for a breath and I said, "I left him rent checks. Three months' worth. Fucking hell."

Masie tilted her head, her brow furrowed like she was trying to piece it all together. "That was the karmic thing to do," she said with an earnest nod.

"I guess," I muttered, wiping my eye with the back of my hand.

She took a slow swig from her beer can, her long black hair catching the last light of the sinking sun. Without another word, she leaned forward, kissed my forehead softly, and turned in for the night.

I dragged myself to a flimsy green chair near the dumpster. My body ached from the day, the kind of exhaustion that sinks into your bones.

I pulled out my phone, and there it was—the text. His name on the screen.

The words turned my stomach as I reread it over and over.

I didn't know how—or if—I should respond, knowing either choice could easily spark an argument.

To him, it seemed like everything I did was wrong.

I'd stay calm and sympathetic, even when he went

completely unhinged.

But it never worked.

I tried to understand where his head was—how, when he was around, I constantly worked to empathize with his situation. Maybe he was just as broken over the fire, feeling helpless or less of a hero because I'd been the one to catch it first, and he was unwilling to admit that. Maybe he resented that my small settlement was already gone, swallowed up by overdue bills and debts. Maybe my settlement was really all I was worth to him. The timing and his demeanor changed vastly once the money was gone—but I didn't understand. I could never use someone like that, but could he?

The fighting progressed. Every small thing became something big.

He gave me hell for using a microwave, installing a 5G router, and we argued about the presidential ballot. This grand divide of disillusionment backed me into a corner—told to put up and shut up.

It's hard feeling like you're hated in your own home, despite giving up everything I knew and loved—to be with him, *to be part of his world*.

Then I'd deny everything.

He loved me; I loved him.

Why would we be together otherwise?

It would get better, I thought. Each and every time.

There had to be a refuge to help me stay. What I needed to feel a lot less alone, hoping to guide me back to the path that I needed to be on. Coming back to calm was always my hope.

So, until then, I'd hide away in music.

"Repo Man" Chevy Malibu gave me a reason to be out the door.

Go somewhere else for a short while.

So it was.

Driving and music. Two elements that forged together to supplement my escape.

In those moments, I felt free. Free of criticism, of landmines—where I could authentically be myself without feeling like I had to look over my shoulder. Where there was no judgment or pain.

This was taking the long way, which at the time, I thought was the right way.

Back in New Mexico, I took the long way to Abiquiu to see the plant organ mountains and the homestead of artist Georgia O'Keeffe, when I stopped in Santuario de Chimayo.

Smack dab in between the capital city and our adobe house, is considered the holiest land in the U.S., akin to the Vatican or Jerusalem. Chimayo claims to have healing dirt, and on the mounds of a nearby creek, a collection of crutches and prosthetic limbs of the healed. Crosses and pieces of prayers taped up, adjacent to the chapel.

The sky was ominous, but the light lifted the clouds to a silver hue.

I purchased a plastic container from the gift shop to gather a bit of blessed dirt. The dirt, 'tierra bendita', is considered holy because it comes from the 'el Pocito', the small pit where Our Lord of Esquipulas's crucifix was discovered in 1810.

I made my rounds and bore witness to those in prayer.

The chapel doors were locked.

Where the hell is this dirt? I mouthed.

The compound was under construction, surrounded by a chain-link fence with torn-up ground beneath it.

I crouched down, dipping the cup into the loose soil and carefully screwing the lid back on.

It didn't matter that I'd later learn the dirt I'd gathered wasn't sacred or holy. At that moment, I wasn't looking for sanctity—I just needed something to believe in. Letting go wasn't easy, and sometimes, a handful of earth felt like the only tangible piece of hope I could carry.

But nothing could've prepared me for what was about to happen when I got home...

My ex and I were driving through the village when he slammed on the brakes, his eyes lighting up with that rare spark, the one that always caught me off guard. Off to the side of the road, a fledgling magpie hopped in the dust, its wings too small, its body too fragile.

He turned to me, his voice alive for once. "I'm taking it," he said, like it was a given, like I'd agree.

"Please leave it," I said quietly. "If your scent gets on it, the mother won't come back."

But he didn't listen. He never listened. Not to me.

He brought it home, cradling it like some kind of prize, and dropped it into a cage. He didn't know what to do next—he never thought that far ahead—thinking YouTube tutorials would do the trick.

He tried feeding it with an eyedropper, his hands too clumsy, too rushed.

The bird twitched, its tiny body jolting once before going still.

He panicked, rolling it, lifeless, in his palms.

He rubbed it, tried warming it with his breath, but it was gone.

The bird was dead.

I said nothing.

I took it.

Its body, weightless.

I carried it out back and dug a hole, sprinkling its body with some of the Chimayo dirt.

I stood back and stared at the tiny mound for some time.

Something so small and so helpless. He decided it was his to take.

WRECKING BALL

PORTLAND, OREGON, 2018. A couple of weeks into dating, my ex told me that he was offered a great job and had to relocate to southern Oregon.

"He wants me to go with him," I told my girlfriend, Allison.

We were sitting in a small café in the Hawthorne district. Worn wicker chairs and tables with mosaic tops, dark drapes framing the windows, and fresh espresso mixing with the tang of mimosas.

Allison brushed a strand of purple hair from her forehead, my reflection mirrored in her black-framed glasses. Her calm yet resolute demeanor seemed to ground the conversation as she said, "Too soon—you just met."

"Dude, he called me his *soulmate*," I replied, half in awe, half in defense.

"Your whole life is in Portland. Your industry, your friends, you went to college here and lived here forever—it's your scene. It's not ideal to give up your life for someone new. Consider long distance first."

Her voice was steady, wrapped in care, trying to anchor me before I'd drift too far away.

But I was hellbent. This was different. I couldn't shake it.

On our first date, he told me how he had an injury like mine. He seemed to understand what it was like pretending everything was okay when it wasn't, or being so exhausted it felt like an acid trip. Brain injuries are lonely, invisible wounds that isolate you in your mind and symptoms.

You lose yourself.

Finding someone who seemed to get it—especially as I was going through it—someone who got the fucked-up notions and endless trials of recovery, was comforting.

It felt like destiny.

So it was easy to tether myself to him, to believe in the bond of shared experience.

My brain was still healing, and everything felt raw and new—every sensation heightened, every moment charged.

Especially falling for someone.

It wasn't a choice; it was instinct. My recovering brain thrived on emotion, clinging to the idea of connection.

Allison sat there, her fingers resting on the edge of her coffee cup, her eyes sharp and knowing. She was weighing her words carefully, as if she knew I wouldn't listen but had put them there as caution. Perhaps my mirror, reflecting the practicality I refused to face.

It was never really in the cards for me to leave. But anyone who believed they'd found someone who truly understood them would have done the same.

I looked at Allison and said bluntly, "He said *long distance never works*."

Her lips pressed into a thin line. I could see what she wanted to say: *Neither will this*.

But she didn't.

She just let me sit in my conviction, offering me silent support through a mild smile of compassion, knowing my mind was already made up.

"Maybe he and I crossed paths before," I said, my voice soft, almost unsure. "In another life... another time. Allison, how will I know if I don't try?"

Everything was him now, the new guy, the man who held me so close with agile limbs, and his beautiful strong hands.

I felt he could recreate me, or create a life with me and save me.

All about him. I would've given anything, everything, whatever I had to.

To never be alone again because this person got me.

This all happened for a reason, and it was to find him, I was sure.

My great love.

One night, while bar hopping, I broke my sobriety despite doctor's orders—a decision I deeply regret, knowing no one with this kind of injury should drink without medical approval. The details of that night were a blur, but I woke up the next morning in his bed, and he told me he'd skipped work to go ring shopping. We stopped for breakfast on the way.

A hipster delight, Nutella and oat milk foam.

The restaurant was busy.

Waiters with thick mustaches, skinny jeans, and teeny-tiny beanies.

When his plate arrived, he looked down at it, his face pasted with an unmistakable snarl. It came with avocado toast. He *hated* avocado toast—such bourgeois fare.

He shoved the plate aside, arms crossed in protest.

"I'm sorry, I picked this place," I said softly, trying to soothe him, my voice tinged with affection despite his disdain. "Do you want something else? We can go somewhere else."

In the end, we sealed the deal with rings and matching tattoos over our hearts—a symbol of the path to enlightenment, marking our commitment to the journey ahead.

Together.

You can't blame someone for getting caught up in a drunken, brain-broke romance, right?

Like when Harry met Sally, *"When you realize you want to spend the rest of your life with somebody, you want the rest of your life to start as soon as possible."*

So in that, my ex and I moved south to a small town that hosted an eclectic mix of Old San Francisco defector hippies, farmers, and city rejects. The downtown, five blocks long, is filled with antique stores and organic restaurants. It's known for its DIY ethos, bridges and yurts.

I made do by cultivating a garden, raising chickens, and fermenting Kombucha. City-girl-gone-country was an interesting story.

Our farmhouse was off the logging roads, locally known as 'the BLM's'. The big four-bedroom rental on eight acres was like being given a big clean slate to build a home together.

We had little money, borrowing from friends and family as needed, while I culled my closet and sold my beloved Squier Vista Venus guitar to help fund the move. I furnished our home for less than a couple hundred between Goodwill and Craigslist, with my collection of '70s dishes, mugs, and amber glassware proudly displayed in the built-in China cabinet.

But the glamor of *Green Acres* was all a front.

We slept on a pallet wood bed frame.

There was no shower and very limited amounts of hot water from rain barrels. We often took baths together until he managed to rig something up with a clasp and hose from Home Depot. I washed the clothes by hand in paint buckets, then hung them out on the line to dry. The internet was a hotspot box where the connection was limited and often nabbed by CB radios and planes overhead.

This was a far cry from what I knew—a pristine vintage studio apartment on Portland's east side, where cocktail hours were marked by Balenciaga bags and pâté crostini after hours of milling around record stores and high-end clothing shops.

But this house was ours, embraced fully because I was building a home with someone—a life so different and real from anything I'd ever known. The property was bordered by firs, with blackberry bushes along the edges and apple trees dotting the yard.

The ten-foot ceilings and random rooms with heat converters affixed. Turn the bedroom off, and turn on the other in my office. Close the door to let it warm up, put on my winter coat and boots.

Make a pot of coffee. Feed the dog, cats.

Walk to the barn to let the goats into the field.

Feed the chickens and gather up the eggs.

Pour my coffee into a thermos.

My breath lingered in the air and my fingertips froze.

Even in my office, still not fully heated, I'd keep my jacket and wool socks on, drape a heated blanket over my lap, and pray for my internet connection to survive.

It was makeshift.

Everything.

We only had one car, and he took it to work every day.

For two years, it was just me—alone at home—all the time.

He left early or slept until two in the afternoon on Mondays and Tuesdays, his days off, while I worked Monday through Friday, so the farm was my responsibility.

But I also traveled for work from time to time.

After that Christmas, I went to Los Angeles. I stopped at the Rainbow Bar and Grill to pour one out for Lemmy Kilmister of Motörhead, then was dropped at the Hollywood Forever Cemetery.

I love L.A. and its long rich history and its myriad of versatile aged glamor against the backdrop of stucco and degrading billboards. Hollywood is a creepy ancient crater; a glitter-bombed and grimy pastel portal, with its infamous cemetery set in between Paramount Pictures and the sign nestled in the hills.

I bought a small bouquet for Soundgarden singer Chris Cornell, whose final resting place is by the lake, across from the grand marble columbarium and neighboring Johnny Ramone. The cemetery was peaceful, with tall palm trees swaying in the breeze and a scattering of reflecting pools shimmering under the afternoon sun. Marble angels and weathered headstones stood as silent guardians over the manicured green lawns, their stillness contrasting with the city beyond its gates.

Chris's site was still adorned with tinsel and Christmas bulbs. I placed the flowers down carefully, their colors vivid against the muted tones of the dark stone. Reaching for my phone, I snapped a photo and cued the track "Say Hello 2 Heaven." I picked up one of the ornaments and slipped the souvenir into my bag—a small piece of the moment to carry with me.

It was late afternoon, and still without a word or text from my ex, I gave in and called him.

I asked, "Why don't I feel like you love me? Despite all of this, why—"

He cut me off, his tone cold and quick. "I don't know. *Why?* That's a question you need to ask yourself. Why don't you feel like I love you?"

I felt a shift, heavy and sharp, as I sat down on a nearby bench. Picking at a blade of grass between my fingers, I struggled to fight back the tears.

"Actions speak louder than words to me," I said, trying to find a way through his wall. "And you have done nothing to make me feel like you love me... I just feel so emotionally separated from you, and I feel like everything is so siloed. It's hard for me to talk to—"

"You're using words that don't make sense," he interrupted, his voice slicing cleanly through mine. "So siloed. What do you mean, *siloed*?"

"Separate," I said, sighing. "Siloed as in separate. It's a euphemism."

"I don't understand euphemisms," he shot back. "I'm a realist. I need to know the facts. I need to know what you're talking about."

"Exactly. That's why you don't understand feelings—you're all about facts," I said, the words pushing forward despite my better judgment. "The fact is, I don't feel like you care about me at all."

"And I ask you why."

"We don't sleep together," I said, the words falling heavy. "You're obviously not attracted to me."

"These sound like your assumptions, not facts," he retorted, his tone mechanical. "You're calling these facts.

These are what you feel."

"And my feelings are valid," I said, feeling the tension rising. "There's nothing wrong with that."

"No, but I don't think *everybody's feelings* are valid."

"Why do you say *feelings* like it's a quotation?" I asked, my voice tinged with frustration.

"Because feelings aren't facts," he snapped.

"If you don't have feelings, you can't be in a relationship," I said, trying to cut his logic with plain truth.

"I understand, and that makes sense, but feelings aren't facts," he said, doubling down.

"Then what do you feel?"

"*No,* don't flip it around," he said sharply. "We gotta finish what you're talking about because you said you don't feel this way. Okay? That doesn't mean things aren't that way. You just don't have enough of it that you want. So that's selfish. You're being selfish."

"I'm being selfish because I want to feel loved?" I asked, my voice trembling between anger and disbelief.

"You're not feeling the love that you want to feel," he said, and then hung up.

There it was: defensiveness, dismissiveness, and dominance—all wrapped in a neat little package of denial.

That phone call left me hollow, yet strangely clear. I realized then that "home" had become an illusion with him.

Being in Los Angeles, though, made me feel closer to a true sense of home than the one I was trying to build. L.A. wasn't just a place—it was an energy, a rhythm I understood. It was where I went to graduate school, worked music gigs, and learned how life could feel alive and brimming with possibility. The city always welcomed me with open arms, like the Santa Ana winds sweeping over Malibu, warm and unpredictable. It had its flaws, but it had a way of giving me exactly what I needed—or thought I needed—at the time.

The men there were no exception.

Once, a short-lived high school Sadie-Hawkins-date-turned-film-editor surprised me with a 2.5-carat black diamond ring. We used to meet up as kids on Friday nights at the roller rink, chasing each other under the fluorescent lights, a blur of wheels and fleeting glances framed by braces. Years later, we crossed paths at a party, the kind of chance encounter that only seems to happen in L.A.—where the past and present collide in such cinematic fashion.

I let myself believe in the grand gesture, in the idea that a moment like that could rewrite everything, erase the loneliness that crept in when the city's glitter faded. The ring wasn't about him—it was about the promise of something larger. It felt like the universe nudging me toward something meant to be. It felt like fate, but fate has many faces.

But L.A., for all its kindness, was also a city of delusion.

And as I held that ring, its weight settling into my palm, I realized that's all it was—an illusion. A dark sparkling symbol of a story I wasn't ready to tell myself was a lie.

So why take the ring? Why entertain the fantasy?

I was following the Hollywood script.

SIDE B

DO YOU LOVE ME NOW?

TIME TICKED ON in Olympia. It was like I never existed. We never existed. Life just carried on, indifferent.

I accepted that it had to end, but my ex kept running. There was no way to chase him either—no path to follow, no way to bridge the distance, just void. It all felt wrong, almost pathetic, to even look for him. Every step in his direction betrayed my dignity.

For someone who never wanted to be found though, free as a bird on the dusty backroads of the U.S., one day turned up tagged in an Instagram photo. In Colorado. Just three hours north of our house in New Mexico. I was shocked to find him so close, after all this time—lingering just beyond my reach, as if he'd been waiting for me to notice.

The photo caption read: *We met this guy who lost his home in the wildfires, he's been living in this travel trailer with his dog ever since.*

I sat up in my chair. "*Ever since*—seriously?"

I messaged the person who made the post, explaining the situation and how I'd been trying to reach him, clinging to a faint hope for some shred of civility.

They responded, saying it 'seemed like he was in a bad headspace' and 'crept around their camp all weekend long'. Then kindly agreed to contact him on my behalf.

Within moments, my phone lit up with a text from my ex: *Why the fuck are you bothering strangers? They are my friends!*

I texted back: *Please just go back to the house and take care of things. I'm all the way back in the Pacific Northwest.*

He texted: *I met awesome people who invited me to spend the weekend with them. Those people said they were grateful to have met me.*

So much for interaction. I wondered how he could carry such an inflated sense of self-importance, an insatiable need for admiration, and such a glaring lack of empathy—for leaving me and the home we shared, behind.

I texted: *Forget it, I'll take care of the house.*

After that, he blocked me and all my friends on social media.

Two weeks later, Hilary and I found ourselves in New Mexico, pulling out of the Santa Fe airport—a tiny, adobe-style building nestled against a backdrop of red cliffs and open desert sky. The scent of sagebrush lingered in the dry, sunbaked air as we made our way to the U-Haul counter, its fluorescent lighting a sharp contrast to the soft, earthy tones outside.

Finding a credit card that would work was the biggest issue. I hadn't yet recouped all the expenses from moving from Oregon to New Mexico, and then to Washington.

The parking lot was nearly empty, save for a scattering of rental cars and the van waiting for us. We had less than forty-eight hours to get everything out of the house.

The sunburst mocked my sadness. "I moved thirteen hundred miles to live here for three months," I said, taking the wheel. "And now we have to drive another hundred miles to empty the fucking house, all because of him."

Her long tawny hair fell back over the seat as she tilted her head, taking a long, slow sip of her Starbucks, the motion unhurried and deliberate. She then reached over and turned on the radio, settling on a station playing Pearl Jam. The opening chords of "Elderly Woman Behind the Counter in a Small Town" filled the cab.

Hilary was my anchor. She could soak up the chaos around her and fly with it to make anyone feel a lot less crazy. "*Fuck him*," she said bluntly, with the kind of reassurance you don't realize you need until it's said out loud.

I texted the landlord, letting them know we'd be coming

up the driveway in a van, so they wouldn't be caught off guard.

It was late by the time we arrived.

We pulled in and they stepped out onto the porch, a soft moonlight spilling out as they stepped into the yard. Silver strands of glittering hair floated over their shoulders.

They opened their arms, I folded in.

Their kindness, effortless and unspoken, softened the shame of letting them down as a tenant. They had been more than understanding, refusing to take rent from someone who no longer lived there and sympathizing with the mess my ex had left behind.

"I am so sorry about this," I murmured, pulling back and wiping my nose against my sleeve, my voice shrouded in remorse. "Please, let me know if there's anything I can do. I feel terrible about everything."

They shook their head, their expression one of genuine empathy. "I'm sorry things turned out the way they did," they said, lingering for a moment before retreating into their home. Then the door closed gently, leaving me with the discomfort of an unfinished goodbye.

Hilary edged toward the house and opened the front door. "Squee!"

Her delight over the rustic flooring, adobe walls, Aztec rugs, and the industrial gas stove broke a smile across her face. Her fingers brushed the turquoise cabinet—eyes lighting up as the charm pulled her in—the rough-hewn beams, the blue kitchen cart, even the buzz of the fridge and scent of aged wood seemed to enchant her as if every detail held its own quiet desert-laden magic.

The line of cacti I'd placed on the windowsill and the deer antler he bought from a roadside vendor sat untouched. In the living room, borrowed furniture mixed with our TV, coffee table, and his knickknacks, including a bronze statue of Ganesha. Once a symbol of wisdom and new beginnings, it now felt hollow—a stark contrast to who he'd become. The open-mindedness and balance it represented clashed with his recent obsession with right-wing politics, a shift that disgusted me. My ex, a man who once spoke of harmony and unity had turned rigid and divisive. I couldn't escape the bitter realization that I'd fallen for a facade.

I picked up Ganesha, stared at it long and hard before dropping it into a box. "Guess this is a good place to start." I hastily pulled the rest of his scattered trinkets in from the shelf, not caring if anything broke from my carelessness.

Each room slowly lost the last traces of life with my ex.

Our movements mechanical and focused, driven by the ticking clock.

Within three hours, Hilary and I boxed up, piled up, and swept up the house.

We grabbed a couple of lawn chairs and settled on the back porch. Hilary lit a cigarette, the glow of the ember flickering in the dark. I watched the smoke curl upward, disappearing into a sky that felt more massive and all-encompassing than ever. We mused about being so close to the edge of the universe.

I looked at Hilary. "Tomorrow, can you drive the trash to the dump down the road, or would you rather wait for the movers?"

Her eyes lit up. "YES! Adventure!" She bounced in her seat, perhaps already revving the task in her mind. Hilary thrived on new tasks, anything that broke up the monotony and gave her a spark of purpose. Her energy was infectious, turning even the most mundane errand into an opportunity for excitement. "Wait—should we stop for snacks before? Or coffee? Oh, wait, do you think the dump smells like? Gross-gross or just trash-gross? Because there's a difference, you know?" She tapped her finger on her knees, words spilling out faster than I could follow.

"It's a *literal* dump," I said, smiling.

"But still, snacks… banana bread!" she said, quickly standing up, ready to go.

By three in the morning, we crashed.

Morning came too soon, the light creeping through the windows to pull us back to reality. Groggy but determined, we threw on yesterday's clothes and set out for coffee, the promise of caffeine the only thing keeping things moving.

The shop was next to a biker bar where, shortly after my ex disappeared, I sat alone on a broken stoop, contemplating my future after finding out about the dental hygienist from Wisconsin. I wondered if he got on the road just to get to her and if he was meeting up with other women along the way.

Back at the house, it was emptied within an hour, leaving only what was there in the first place. My entire life was gone again, in boxes again, shipped off again, starting over again.

On the way out of the village, I dropped the meager amount of belongings he left behind, addressed to his mother, at the post office.

Back through the range of brown, down through the valley and up again, we landed for the night at my beloved hotel, El Rey Court, as a welcome reprieve.

The rain began as we hauled our bags inside, soft at first but gaining rhythm, tapping against the windows like a metronome for our exhaustion. We didn't bother with anything fancy—just McDonald's for dinner and a drink to unwind.

Hilary, thinking herself a cocktail savant, cracked open a bottle of Jalapeño Pineapple Margarita. Not knowing it was perfectly pre-mixed, she topped it off with a generous pour of 400 Conejos mezcal.

"This is *so good*," she said, her hand flapping wildly at me.

She handed me a glass. Rich, smokey, with the perfect bite of sour.

We downed glasses and she poured two more, then three—each one better than the last.

Hilary inhaled the drink in two swift chugs before slamming down the empty glass.

She pulled out her phone. "*I should call him*, he'll pick up."

I froze mid-bite, my burger hovering inches from my mouth and said, "I won't stop you."

Maybe it was the efflux of adrenaline, the fact that we were rushing in and out of New Mexico with tightened tasks at hand, but when he answered, it was all too obvious—we were shitfaced.

Muffled against Hilary's face, I could hear his voice on the other end of the receiver.

She took a breath and then exploded—

"What the fuck do you think you're doing you're a liar and a cheater and you ruined her life you fuckin' narcissist don't even take responsibility for your actions you fuckin' jerk you hurt her and took advantage of her and we all see right through you you fucking stonewalling prick she loved you and you suck—ASSHOLE!"

He hung up.

Hilary stood there, her anger still radiating.

She looked at me and tossed the phone on the bed.

I have never heard Hilary yell, not a day before that moment and not since.

That final exchange made him disappear completely.

SWALLOW MY PRIDE

The Oregon wildfires of 2020 consumed over a million acres, marking one of the most destructive natural disasters in the state's history. When it happened, it was still the winter of absolution around the globe with no COVID vaccine yet readily available, mask mandates, and six-feet social distancing intact. Restrictions were all too slowly being lifted to help move humanity into some form of normalcy. The Biden-versus-Trump election blanketed the nation like a tarp over a transmissionless car that sat untouched in a driveway far too long. The fire was a red and blue savior—the alleged dispute between the state and Feds—and those conspiracy theorists who believed chem trails were the source of all corruption. One side said "let the fucker burn", and the other implemented the old Vietnam tactic of cloud seeding as the fires hovered on city limits. There were whispers from Red Cross volunteers as campaigners swooped in for their big publicity shot. One side had been dipping their hands into donation buckets to compensate for the lack of fundraising, or so it was rumored.

Awaiting news of our house as the stagnant toxic plume sat over the city, any variation of loss hadn't registered, even when I was holding dented cans of food from the relief center. Pitying myself would be the biggest failure; though I felt pain for others who were displaced with their children and lost homes that had been in their families for generations.

When the firefighters were finally able to put out the blaze, I didn't even consider for a second to step foot on the property. Word came through in a Facebook message while I was standing outside a Famous Footwear with a box of boots. I had to verify property information— because there were looters—to add insult to injury.

The parking lot was alive with motion. Cars weaving through lanes, carts clattering over pavement, and passing voices rising and falling in fragments. Yet, it all seemed muted, like the world had turned the volume down. Even car engines and the shuffle of footsteps felt far away, as if I stood still in the center of a whirlwind, disconnected. The stillness wasn't in the space—it was in me, a quiet pause in the middle of so much noise.

I looked up at the sky from the concrete lot and took a breath.

Everything was destroyed.

There was nothing left to do but move on.

I had to.

Plain and simple.

An empire can't be rebuilt from ash.

I was collecting, scanning, and delivering receipts for the items we were trying to recoup after the fire, filing paperwork to prove residency, and scrambling to gather personal records from the government. I was still working hard—planning, pushing forward, making meals—doing everything I could to keep us afloat.

And all the while, my ex slept.

The stress of handling it all alone was crushing.

In the late hours, I buried myself in television, mainly the show *Married at First Sight*, where strangers are paired up by 'experts' as part of an experiment. The couples meet at the altar and are expected to expedite a manufactured relationship where they ultimately decide to stay married or get a divorce after just two months together. I was watching it when my ex returned home from surveying the property.

He presented me with a broken piece of my favorite red coffee mug.

The last piece of my former life. A single chunk of ceramic.

"We should buy the property outright," he said enthusiastically. "We can live in a trailer. The land will grow back green from the ashes and soot."

The suggestion cut deeper than he probably realized. "I'm never going back there."

Silence settled between us.

I exhaled sharply, unable to stop the flood of words. "You didn't want me to pay the sixty dollars for the insurance. You said no. *We don't need insurance. No, the house isn't burning down. No, we don't have to leave.* Did you not? Did you not say that we didn't have to leave?"

His hands formed into fists and his knuckles pressed hard against the granite countertop. "First of all, no—I didn't want to leave because, as the man of the house, I felt like I should protect it. Second, insurance? We said we were going to get it. There were no questions about the cost. Don't lie about that, because that makes you a liar."

I bristled, the words hitting me like a slap. "I'm not a liar. You didn't want to pay the sixty dollars for the insurance. I said *fuck that*."

His voice sharpened as he straightened up. "No, you're lying. That never happened."

"It did happen! Just like you didn't want to leave the house. It happened!"

"No," he said, his tone icy. "You're lying—that is a lie."

"It's not a lie."

"You made that up in your brain," he accused.

I smacked my forehead, the frustration bubbling over. "Don't gaslight me. I know the facts."

"Gaslight?" He scoffed. "Do you even know what gaslighting means?"

"Yes," I said, my voice rising. "It means making someone question their reality, making them doubt what they know to be true."

"Wrong," he snapped. "Gaslighting is creating something out of nothing. That's exactly what you're doing right now."

I refused to let him twist the narrative anymore. "We were sitting on the bed at the hotel, and I said we should get insurance because you didn't. I handed you my card and said, '*Let's just fucking do it.*' You seemed apprehensive—just like you were about leaving the house."

He looked down, his shoulders sagging. "So you're going to hold that against me forever? That makes you a mean person."

My jaw tightened. "You didn't want to leave."

"I didn't," he admitted, his voice softer now. "Because I wanted to defend my house. Am I not allowed to be a little proud that I wanted to save you and everything?"

"You didn't save me," I said, my voice trembling with anger and disbelief. "If I hadn't woken up, we'd be dead."

DON'T WORRY

I MET UP with Blondie to break the news I was moving to Pittsburgh. We were on a restaurant patio overlooking the opposite end of Capitol Lake Park, toward my apartment in Olympia. Lakefair was that weekend. Immobile carnival rides and stands were set up, their pinks, blues, and whites scattered across the park like litter on the grass.

Life at an amusing standstill.

Blondie leaned on the backrest, her platinum cropped hair perfectly in place. She swirled her wine glass with deliberate precision. The flash tattoos scattered across her arms—small, sharp symbols with thick lines and clean designs proudly exposed—pieces of a story she didn't care if anyone read. Her expression, as always, was flat and matter-of-fact. Her features made even her silence feel like a big-ass bold statement.

"Might be good. Then again, when we move off our path, the universe is disrupted," she said, setting down and then lifting another glass from the wine taster. She studied it like she could glean the meaning of life from it. "Everything goes wrong until we get it right. If everything is right, it's easy. And you're never about easy, are you?"

I stared at the fair in the distance. Somehow, it seemed louder than the buzz surrounding us.

"When I moved to Olympia it seemed like a good idea," I said, "But as comforting as it is, I can't stay here forever. I need something different. Something that feels like forward motion."

"Going back home though, to PA?" Blondie set the glass down with a soft clink. "But let me guess—you've spent weeks agonizing about this and now feel guilty because the universe didn't come down and send you a written invitation to leave."

"Not exactly," I said, hesitating. "But I never thought about whether I was ready to leave. I just feel like I have to. Right now. Olympia isn't... I'm not... I'm just... rotting at The Brotherhood, night after night."

Blondie arched a brow, her expression giving nothing away. "Then go," she said simply. "This time, starting over is for you and no one else. You don't have to justify it, not to me *or you* or anyone the fuck else."

Her calm threw me for a second, but something deep down gnawed at me. "Speaking of starting over, after the fire, things got weird," I said, the words tripping up before I could stop them.

Blondie tilted her head, her lips twitching into a faint smirk. "Weird like how?"

"My sister convinced me I needed protection."

She rolled her eyes. "Oh, *GOD*. Here we go."

"Her spiritual guide said I should realign my chakra and smudge sage daily to ward off bad spirits," I said. "I started braiding my hair, wearing a Hamsa and Saint Christopher, and carrying tourmaline and quartz in my pocket." I hesitated, then added, "—oh, and I got an email from my baby's daddy the day before the fire—my sister swears it was the catalyst."

Blondie set her glass down again, this time with fervor. "Wait. Let me get this straight. You get one bad-energy email from baby daddy, *and poof*, the forest burns down?! *That's your sister's* take?"

"Pretty much."

"Right. Because *clearly*, he holds the keys to universal destruction," she said, deadpan. "Thousands of acres of land wiped out because he fired off a half-assed email. Makes *total sense*." She paused, taking a measured sip of her wine, then added, "Maybe the fire had nothing to do with him, and she just thinks he's an asshole—ever think of *that*?"

Her words were so matter-of-fact, so cutting yet

somehow kind, that I couldn't help but laugh.

"*What?!* I'm just *saying*," she added with a shrug, her eyes steady. "Not everything in the universe revolves around one guy's bad vibes. It's bullshit."

I shook my head, smiling. Blondie had a way of making everything feel simultaneously absurd and manageable, like she was calmly resetting the balance of the world with every sharp, simple truth.

She tilted her glass in my direction. "*Anyway*, if the gods of bad emails strike again, just text me. I'll be here—different patio, different drinks maybe, but here... You get it."

Leaving Olympia was like stepping offstage mid-set—abrupt, awkward, but necessary—and with overwhelming feedback. That town, on an endless vinyl loop, had carved itself into me, one groove at a time. But there's only so long you can live in a place before it starts to crack and echo back all the things you're trying to forget.

The following week I left.

It was sunny, summer, with clear skies that made life in Olympia feel strangely unfamiliar.

On the street, parked beside a meter, I crammed my entire life into a single moving container.

No fanfare, no teary sendoff.

I fell fugue. Donning flannel would've given me enough incentive to stay if it had been closer to fall. I would've just gone to Tacoma to play pinball for an hour instead of making a journey back east.

I felt like a failure somehow.

Olympia in the rearview felt more like a slow yet inevitable shift further from grace.

On the first leg of the drive, Mount Rainier loomed. Sharp, blue, imposing, as if it wanted to follow me, towering and constant.

For a while, it felt like it did.

Each turn in the road wound around more edges of mountain shadows, stubborn accompaniment as if trying to pull me back.

But it had to be done.

The Pacific Northwest scenery faded, albeit little by little. High skies to red rocks and eventually what replaced any sense of adventure were the long flattened Midwest plains.

I was in the wide-open nothingness of Nebraska, where the land dragged out, went on forever and without a break. At least in the mountains, you know what you're up against. Further east, there's nothing to push against but the horizon, and it doesn't fight back—it just keeps going. Middle America held its own kind of noise that made every memory sharper, every loss more immediate.

My thoughts like a scratched CD, skipping back to life

with my ex—a relentless racket of familiar tracks soaked in nostalgia and regret.

Every note, every flaw.

The sound of what was—and what we'd lost—cut through.

It was a tired racket.

All the rest stops were the same. Gas stations with old cold fried chicken buckets. Parking lots dotted with weary travelers in search of cell reception. I stopped only when I had to.

With a playlist titled 'Another Year Down', I turned my thoughts to what could be.

"It's my party and I'll cry if I want to."

Pittsburgh wasn't the dream, but it was somewhere. Built on the ashes of industry, on steel and smoke, Andy Warhol popism and punk—whatever the hell makes a place thrive or unbreakable. It felt like the kind of place where someone like me could disappear for a while—or rebuild.

I tried to picture myself there.

Disappearing.

Scanning the rows of Mister Rogers Neighborhood. Bridges and brick buildings stretched over brackish rivers, their edges softened by the ravines of the Allegheny. A city with its own scars—jagged and unapologetic. It mirrored the state of my life, my heart.

I could stop pretending.

Pittsburgh wouldn't ask me to be anything.

Maybe I'd start a revolution from my bed.

SHELTER SONG

MY APARTMENT, WITH its mustard-colored furniture and afghans, was a garish gray Victorian on the corner of the Shadyside gayborhood. The chipped wood floors, small bathroom, and kitchen fit perfectly with my static rerun aesthetic. The faint smell of stale cigarettes clung to the walls, grounding me in a strange kind of familiarity.

Pittsburgh was a new kind of acculturation, with a massive influx of Brooklyn and Manhattan defectors settling in since the pandemic, changing the landscape of such a familiar place. Pennsylvania was where my life began, but in the seventeen years since I'd left, everything had been rearranged, as if struggling to adapt to its own new identity.

I eavesdropped on the girl downstairs and watched the maple trees blink through the white lace curtains in my bedroom.

It resembled a home, but it wasn't.

Not yet.

But maybe, just maybe, it could've been.

I wanted to make it work.

I had to.

I'd accumulated too much stuff.

Depression they say. Dopamine hits in packages and placeholders. Objectified.

My closet was full of clothes, I had furniture and a full set of dishes, appliances—a fully stocked life that, on paper, looked complete. With each relationship that ended or a move I made, I left everything behind except a pile of clothing, a Tupperware box of small keepsakes, a crate of records, and my guitar. They were the constants in my life, the things I couldn't leave, even when I left everything else.

Owning things was never *my thing*.

I absolutely wasn't prepared for the daunting task of walking into a department store after the fire. When you need everything, it's nearly impossible to decide what's most important. Socks, underwear, toothpaste, and a toothbrush come to mind—but what about the creature comforts? The tiny luxuries that make life feel normal? A ten-dollar coffee maker and a fourteen-dollar bag of Blue Bottle Coffee beans seem like a good start, but then you need a grinder, filters, and maybe even a scoop if you're as meticulous as I am. And of course, a mug to pour it into.

But what about all the other things? The irreplaceable

things? Old photos, art created, birthday cards from dead grandparents. These belongings were never coming back, so I had to make do with necessities. Yet I'd pick up a bar of soap at the grocery store and sob.

How could I ever buy or own or keep anything ever again?

The thought of *Antiques Roadshow, Storage Wars,* and *American Pickers* pissed me off.

People with stuff.

The value of stuff.

Stuff in general.

How could anyone keep things forever, pass them down through time and generations, have so much crap it just sits around and collects dust to the point where it forms sentience?

What's a relic?

What's garbage?

Think about a house, what goes inside of it, every nook and cranny. Each room has its own set of furniture and necessities.

It's just filler.

All of it.

Someone's future thrift find.

But when my childhood best friend, Lacey, said she had my dress, I immediately responded, "*What dress?*"

"Your dress. From high school," she said casually over the phone, like we'd just been talking about it. Her voice was light.

I frowned. "You're gonna have to be more specific."

"Oh, come on, Miss. *The dress*. Purple, polyester, spaghetti straps, black nylon overlay. The one with the little white ruffles at the top. You called it your *Courtney* dress."

I sat up straighter, my brain racing. "*The* baby doll dress?"

"Yes," she said, her tone nonchalant.

Reserved and kind, Lacey and I had met on the school bus in fifth grade. We became fast friends by copying each other's homework assignments and sharing a Walkman loaded with Aerosmith's *Get a Grip*, a tape that we eventually wore out from overplay. During those thirty-minute rides to school and back, our friendship blossomed into something that felt like it would last forever. From elementary school well into high school, we swapped clothes, traded issues of *Hit Parader*, talked boys, and frequented Hot Topic. Concerts and overnights, proms and virginities, smoking cigarettes and drinking coffee—our lives revolved around music. My life revolved around our friendship. But then, junior year, she met AJ, a bass player in a local metal band.

After graduation, I couldn't bear the thought of leaving home—or her—so I stayed behind and enrolled in the local community college. She went to cosmetology school. But our "ride or die" was quickly offed when she got pregnant and married AJ.

Suddenly, there were no more late nights at Perkins, no more concerts or double dates. It was just me—reading graphic novels and listening to CDs alone.

It felt like my first real loss.

My first major life change.

I'd considered her my family.

A couple of years later, I forged my path to Portland, while her life became wrapped up in her relationship and family. Mine unraveled in missteps on a book page.

Pulling myself out of the memory, I said, "I don't remember letting you borrow that dress,"

"You did," she said. "Senior year. You let me borrow it because it looked better on me. You couldn't fill it out anyway and had to wear a black Nine Inch Nails shirt over it."

"Oh, my short-lived goth phase! I remember the boots—the knee-high combat ones! They were so chunky and always got stuck under the gas pedal of my shitty red Chevy."

"You wore that outfit every day for like, a month," she said. "Then went back to your grunge thing."

The memories flickered back in flashes. "How the hell do you still have it?"

"It's yours. It belongs to you," she said, her tone suddenly serious. "I'm preserving history over here. You should be thanking me."

"For stealing my dress?"

"*Borrowing* it," she corrected.

"Full circle, baby!" I shot back, my voice warm with familiarity.

She laughed and said, "That dress deserves a comeback."

A week later, a package arrived at my doorstep, enclosed in a pink bubble mailer scrawled with her unmistakable handwriting. Inside was the dress—still intact, still as striking as I remembered.

It fit better this time around.

I threw it on, draped it with my best shag coat, paired it with muted nude lipstick and taupe eyeshadow, and headed out to see a Danish band I loved—the same band that wrote a power pop ballad I had played on repeat after my ex left.

Those song lyrics calmed me, weaving together the highs and lows, the crashes and burns, the rights and wrongs that I swore, inexplicably, held my truth—offering a sliver of consolation after the ghosting. The least I could do was buy their singer-songwriter a drink as a thank you for his song helping me forage through such a dark period.

I caught up with the band at Gooski's on Polish Hill—a

dive bar well-known for its pierogi and killer curated jukebox. A smokey confection of the local punk and metal scenes. Scrawled walls of graffiti and low red lights harkened a hunger for danger.

The singer requested a Heineken.

He had an ethereal, almost otherworldly quality about him—his pale skin contrasted with the tousled, dark strands of hair that framed his face, and his piercing expression carried both intensity and vulnerability. He wore a worn suede jacket over a patterned shirt, the collar slightly undone, giving him the essence of someone effortlessly cool yet haunted.

I set the beer down, slid into the seat across from him, and leaned in. "That song helped me get through the end of things."

He put his forehead against mine, his voice low and firm. "I didn't write about your relationship. My songs have their own meaning."

"But once art is released into the world, it doesn't belong to you anymore," I said, holding his attention. "This was my interpretation, and it saved me—take it as a win."

Connecting on a level that might be very far from the creator's reality and purpose for release, music was my connection to the universe, and myself. Beyond this, there was no music in Pittsburgh, at least nothing compelling enough for me to remember.

Melvins stopping in once a year wasn't enough to bring me joy. Between Wiz Khalifa, Taylor Swift, and Kenny Chesney, my passion was a foreign agent.

Some call Pittsburgh "Upper West Virginia". The past feels more alive than the present—the same stubborn pride in its bones, just with fewer mountains. The faded industry, narrow one-way streets, and rough-edged charm feel like cousins to the hollers and coal towns to the south. It's a place where history clings to everything, where resilience is woven into the skyline and the accents, and where the boundary between city and country blurs, unapologetic and unrefined.

I don't care for football, the Steelers, or the Miller Lite-guzzling hangers-on that came with it all. French fries don't belong on salad and not everything should come with a side of ranch dressing. No one had as many tattoos, and few people I knew in the city held a substantial job. They all seemed to just be floating among the mire, day by day, sailing on styrofoam boxes and dumpster furniture. Living for the day, lasting for a moment, expecting nothing from life except the distractions in front of them.

I came in with hope, waited for the memories of innocence to resurface.

My soft recollection of the long temperate summers

under the Eastern Hemlocks, hanging under the trestle by the lake; the simple joys of the street fair, where we wore bright striped Dr. Suess hats made of felt and collected chunky resin rings—The Marshall Tucker Band buzzing from our parents' boombox speakers, always. When it all turned to fall, throw on long underwear over a ripped pair of jeans. We rebelled by dying our hair with Kool-Aid and eating giant Pixie Stix under the bleachers at football games—all while wearing Kurt Cobain memorial t-shirts.

We were just kids. Kids left to our own devices.

I found myself feeling lonelier than I did back then.

With my parents in Florida instead of at work and my friends scattered in different directions, I felt just as lost as when I'd moved to southern Oregon with my ex—and later, when he left me behind in New Mexico. I had no connection to anything. Maybe I thought returning to some level of simplicity would trigger a hard reset, granting me a do-over.

Some things felt familiar, but what set me apart from the place where I'd grown up was the simple truth: I'd seen too much. I wasn't a kid anymore.

All I had was time—time to sit, think, waste, and replay.

The past. The present. No future.

Every Friday night, I ate pizza and played Tetris alone. I drifted between a sushi restaurant around the corner and Tina's bar in Bloomfield, its ambiance a faint echo of

Seattle—tinned fish and skin-contact wine, sediment resting in the punt.

Six months turned into a year.

A year turned into two.

No friends, no notable moments—just an endless string of unremarkable days.

I sat and sulked, counting the cracks in the filigree-imprinted walls—in a state of paralysis—my ex's ghosting circled over and over in my mind. What my ex did, he did to me. It was all circumstantial, not because I'd done anything wrong. But nothing would change until I chose to change it. I had to admit I'd become so broken down by him—his actions—that no matter what I did, I could only move forward once I accepted that I was a victim.

I was a victim of his narcissism.

A victim of the fire.

Vulnerable in the fragile state of my recovery.

Damaged, truly, by one thing after another.

I was raised to suck it up, to take care of myself, no matter what.

So I did what I was taught—I sat with it.

I thought long and hard.

I listened to music.

But music wasn't enough. Not this time. It had to be more tangible. Somehow.

The only bonus to living on the East Coast is everything being so close together. Most flights from Pittsburgh to cities like New York and Miami are cheap, and take no more than two hours—a drive to DC, Baltimore, Buffalo, and four to five hours to Detroit Rock City.

A ritual began back in Washington, where I regularly left stargazer lilies for Andy Wood—a quiet tribute that carried me through some of my darkest days.

Not long after, I threw my ring into the Muddy Banks of the Wishkah, where Kurt Cobain slept. His last home in Seattle, nestled next to Viretta Park, had always been one of my favorite places to visit. During one trip, I found an amethyst rock left on one of the graffitied benches—a symbol of protection, clarity, and transformation. It deftly reflects a journey of confronting challenges, transforming them into creative expression, and leaving behind a legacy of authenticity, depth, and resilience.

I thought about all the Seattle musicians who passed. I thought about Mia Zapata.

Finding that rock felt significant, symbolizing the emotional symbiosis between Kurt and Mia's lyrics and their charged performances. Kurt had once told Mia she was a 'great fucking singer.' Their bands shared bills, and Nirvana even played at her benefit concert (as did Pearl Jam and Soundgarden). For years, I'd wanted to visit Mia

Zapata's grave, and it felt like the perfect totem to take to her—an offering in honor of our quiet grief collective.

Now, living close enough to Louisville, Kentucky, I finally had the chance to close the circle, serving as a conduit between two lost souls.

Summer arrived and I drove south to visit her headstone. Nestled in the thick grass, it was just a speck among countless others. There were two sets of wilted flowers and a browned dried card from a local detective, which I pocketed. I laid down a fresh bouquet of yellow roses and set the amethyst over the etching, *Mia Katherine Zapata, August 25, 1965 - July 7, 1993: Cherished Daughter - Sister - Friend - Git.*

Following the tragic loss of their friend, Gretta Harley and Valerie Agnew, fueled by grief and determination, joined forces with other women in the Seattle community to establish Home Alive—an organization dedicated to fostering safety and empowerment. Home Alive offered self-defense classes and equipped individuals with tools to protect themselves and prevent violence. To support their mission, they developed educational curricula and produced a compilation CD featuring local bands. With the support of feminist icon Joan Jett, they even put on powerful benefit shows and recorded the tribute album *Evil Stig*, their efforts standing as a testament to the resilience of a community united by a shared purpose—for Mia.

Sitting by Mia's grave, leaning over her headstone, I cried. I played The Gits' cover of "A Change Is Gonna Come" and quietly thanked her for the music that had carried me through—the fire, the blue nights, and everything in between.

I mused about Carl Jung, the psychologist and pioneering theorist, who famously said, "Who looks outside, dreams; who looks inside, awakes." But what happens when you do both and find nothing on either side?

We rarely see things clearly until we're on the outside looking in.

Then we look outside for validation of our own beliefs.

In that moment, more than in any private encounter I'd had with musicians, even those long gone, I felt the strength in the lasting marks they'd left behind.

I carried on, to Nashville, to pay my respects to Johnny and June Carter Cash.

And when I finally stood before my reflection in the countless mirrors of Elvis's Graceland, in Memphis, the reason I had been moving, and kept on moving, came even further into focus—

Perched on the staircase, I leaned over the riser oh so slightly to get a better look at the rooms Elvis lived among. Eames furniture. A salvaged natural wood coffee table. Green shag carpet moved up from the floor to the ceiling and thick paneled walls. The yellow-brown floral panels were draped over each window, with a quarter shade of white from the dawning December light. I was standing in Elvis's living room—lovingly referred to as the "Jungle Room"—not a soul in sight.

Priscilla Presley was only a freshman in high school when she was swept away by Elvis, who had been drafted to Germany shortly after his fame set in. Once discharged, he requested she join him in Tennessee to finish school, appointing his father Vernon as her legal guardian. He often sprinted to Hollywood to make a series of disastrous films alongside budding starlets whom he had liaisons with, leaving the impressionable Priscilla isolated at home alone with his grandmother and father. Despite the headlines of potential affairs, Priscilla popped the pills and stood quietly by her man. She became pregnant with Lisa Marie, and then Elvis refused to have sex with her after giving birth. However, in claiming he loved her, even long after Priscilla left to engage in her path, she never married again, in fear that Elvis would organize a hit on her potential lovers, as he often threatened.

The rockstars, the players—the romanticized versions of their egos and art—loomed large, overshadowing everything. Yet their music shaped how I saw the world, fueling a misanthropic streak and a disdain for societal norms that colored every choice I made.

All stars eventually fade.

Their impact, though, remained—something to hold on to.

Visiting the homes, graves, and sacred places of musicians began to ground me, bridging the gap between their fading light and my restless momentum. Each stop on the journey offered a sense of purpose—maybe even a sense of home.

But between pilgrimages, life felt stagnant, and my money stretched thin. Staying in or going out felt equally futile unless I wanted to marinate in bar-laced cigarette smoke.

So I found my rhythm on the road to Youngstown, heading north to reconnect with the people and places that shaped everything I knew about music.

The neon glow of West Side Bowl became a refuge, a time capsule, where nearly two decades of rock'n'roll nostalgia clung to a moment that felt frozen in time.

Maybe I went there to feel tethered to something familiar, or maybe it was just the cheapest escape I could find. But somewhere along the way, I realized I wasn't just passing through—I was running. Not toward anything, but away from everything in any way I could.

One fleeting post-teenage past boyfriend behind the bar,

another seated across from me, Ray.

Ray—the guitarist who once could have passed for an Abercrombie model, instead sat in joggers and a sandy Fu Manchu, looking like someone who'd traded ambition for comfort. His laid-back demeanor fit, but there was something faintly adrift about him. Ray and I had shared a college romance that lingered in the corners of my life for nearly a decade before settling into one of the most authentic friendships I'd ever known. He was my first real boyfriend after high school, the one who unknowingly defined the kind of love I'd search for in everyone who came after him.

Looking back, I'd been lucky with love—good boyfriends, mostly amicable endings over the years.

Ray was living proof.

We broke up because I wanted more from life, and he never once resented me for it. In many ways, he helped me realize what I deserved—someone who could grow with me, not hold me back, and not be a dick about it.

Sitting in the bowling alley, I thought about how far I'd come from the restless searching of my early days. Time alone—inside my head and my life—had taught me what I'd outgrown and what I still needed.

"You know what I hate, Miss?" Ray said, leaning forward like he was about to deliver something profound.

"What?"

"Hoarding," he said, practically spitting the word. "Non-working stuff, specifically. Guitar busted? Trash. Amp fried? Trash. Start over."

Ray was a gear nut, so the anecdote hardly surprised me. He always liked things functional, even when the rest of his life didn't seem to follow the same logic. Somehow, he always knew how to hit close to home without me saying a word, his observations landed without feeling intentional.

I laughed, shaking my head. "You'd lose it at Graceland."

"Graceland?" He tilted his head. "Like Elvis?"

"Yeah," I said. "I liked it, but it was... strange. It's like he's about to walk back in at any second. It felt like someone pressed pause forever."

Ray leaned back, thinking. "Yeah, see? That's what I mean. That kind of stagnation? Weird as hell. It's like a museum of not letting go. Who wants to hold on to a place where the guy died on a toilet?"

"That's not the intention," I said.

"Exactly," he said, pointing at me. "But stagnation is anxiety fuel. I look at stuff like that and think, move on already."

"Same," I said. "But I still kind of loved it—the kitsch—I'd go back."

He swirled his leftover swill. "Speaking of, how long are

you going to keep bouncing from place to place?"

I frowned. "What's that supposed to mean?"

"You're running. I get it. But you're not landing anywhere. Portland's where you should be, right? Why not just go back?"

I stayed quiet, picking at my pizza crust.

"It's not that deep," he said after a moment. "Pittsburgh doesn't fit you. You've always hated this whole area, admit it. The cusp of PA and Ohio isn't it."

My silence said it all.

"There!" He nodded, leaning forward. "Portland's more your speed. And at least the strippers there probably know who Elliott Smith is."

I blinked, laughing despite myself. "What?"

"Ohio strippers don't know Elliott Smith," he said, completely serious. "I had to explain who he was to one once. Awkward." Ray raised his glass, a toast to his own absurdity.

The conversation drifted, the kind of comfortable chaos only close friends could manage, but his words about Portland lingered. They hung heavy, wrapped in his usual nonsense but still enough to keep my attention.

On the TV, a grainy Sonic Youth video flickered.

"Pittsburgh isn't my home," I said finally, pulling a pickle off my pizza and setting it aside. "Will you help me drive back?"

Ray touched his chin, his silver signet ring glinting. "To Portland, Absolutely," he said, without hesitation. "But only because their strippers there know who Elliott Smith is."

MAMA, I'M COMING HOME

THE FINAL NIGHT my ex and I spent together, I prepared tuna steaks with pink peppercorn, mashed potatoes, and asparagus for dinner. I presented him with the plate as he sat in front of the television, his face dimly lit by the glow of a late-night show.

I never thought that would be the last time I'd see him.

Earlier that day, we had visited a small ski resort town near the Colorado border. Below the dry slopes, on a sprawled-out blanket, the land endlessly rugged and raw, with mountain goats grazing in the distance.

"You're really going," I said, my voice catching in my throat.

He half-smiled. "Not forever, just a little camping trip."

As we sat on that blanket, I thought about the beginning: the time we took photos kissing in Laurelhurst Park, the way we would return there to reminisce as if revisiting a sacred memory.

I thought of vegan Thanksgiving casseroles, waking up too early but content to watch him sleep, his chest rising and falling in slow, deliberate rhythms.

For those moments, I had felt like a real human being in real love. A family.

But those moments were threads in a tapestry that unraveled quickly.

Though he was right next to me, the distance between us felt immeasurable.

The bad moments outweighed the good. The good moments, though few, strung me up with denial, leaving me clinging to something that no longer existed. What remained of me was a vessel—holding on, letting go, circling endlessly in hope and disillusionment. Both of us had been putting on fronts, masks that now seem painfully obvious in hindsight.

The week before he left, I called Maggie, a childhood friend who had moved to Los Angeles. I was sitting in a historic downtown landmark, an old meeting hall that had once catered to travelers moving along trade routes by carriage. The space was cavernous, its walls adorned with portraits of Native Americans, their expressions solemn and forlorn, almost knowing as they watched..

"I made arrangements to talk with an attorney," I told her, my eyes fixed on the table, tracing patterns in the grain. "If he takes this trip, I'll feel safer and can avoid a blowout. I can't stop thinking about how things might escalate."

Maggie sighed on the other end, her voice steady. "With how many times you've called and texted me about this, you need to protect yourself. You're doing the right thing. Remember what happened to FKA Twigs with Shia LeBeouf? She said he was abusive and even imprisoned her. It cost her forty grand just to get away from him. You don't need to wait for things to get worse before you act."

Her words landed heavily, the weight of them reverberating in the empty hall. The thought of needing that kind of escape, that kind of courage, weighed on me.

Before I could respond, the line went dead. Maggie never was one to linger on words when action was the answer.

I sat there, alone in the gloam, pushing around the ornamental enchiladas on my plate with my fork.

The thick stained-glass windows captured the southwest sky's blaze, casting broken light over my face.

A man stepped onto the stage and began strumming an acoustic guitar, his fingers moving deftly as he plucked the opening notes of Ryan Bingham's award-winning song, "The Weary Kind," written for the 2010 film *Crazy Heart*.

The tune droned like a funeral knell, the melody sinking.

Still.

That day lingers—heavy, unmoving, seared in my memory.

I left Portland for love, first to southern Oregon, then to

New Mexico. Despite everything, I tried to save my relationship, clinging to the glimmers of the beginning. But the magic of 'love at first sight' quickly rendered a sharp reality. They say love is blind, but in abuse, the fear of leaving outweighs the fear of staying.

Fear of the unknown. Fear of retribution. Fear of failing to try hard enough.

So I stayed.

No one builds a home to break it.

No one falls in love thinking of an end.

No one thinks they're going to get hurt.

Hurt kept me there. I thought staying meant love—loneliness, suffering, all of it. For better or for worse. I believed that until the universe screamed otherwise. When my world burned, it sent me a wolf. It collected my friends, pulling them into a story they never asked for, all to save me—because they loved me.

Family, for me, was never traditional.

As a child, it lived in TV screens and daydreams; as an adult, nothing nuclear ever felt real.

I wasn't conventional anyway.

Finding my way back was never going to be a straight line, so astrology became a guide when cosmic shifts felt personal. March's Libra eclipse gave me the courage to break free from disempowering beliefs, and April's Aries eclipse illuminated rebirth. In all the woo-woo, I'd hoped that it would reshape me, reclaim the strength I'd lost, and accept the obvious.

My house burned.

My relationship ended.

Shit happens.

I gave my therapist the cliff notes: "We met not long after my head injury. Moved off the grid with spotty internet. He'd leave me alone for hours, yell all the time, hit on my best friend, and ghosted me when I caught him talking to other women online."

Her voice calm, she replied, "Yeah, people ghost because they want to stay in control and avoid taking responsibility. From what you're telling me, this guy had a pattern—being dismissive, lacking empathy, and using people for his own benefit. Honestly, men like that often target strong, independent women when they're at their most vulnerable. It's classic narcissistic abuse."

With that, I made my move.

No more hesitation, no second-guessing.

I packed and returned to Portland—my real home.

In a new apartment, the life I'd built was waiting to be reclaimed.

I swapped the white "Repo Man" Chevy Malibu for a blue

"Number One Baddie" Ford Bronco and hit the road, heading down to southern Oregon. The freeway drew out under a heat wave. Moving closer to the forest, riding along the scenic byway, the fire signs were red—high danger.

Ozzy Osbourne's "Mama, I'm Coming Home" played on the radio.

I passed children playing in the river, fishermen casting lines, and paddle boarders gliding through the water. The bottom of the ravine was green, but just a few meters above, the charred remains of trees stood like upright metal rakes.

I pulled onto the covered bridge leading to the house, thinking about how, if it had burned, we would have never made it out.

Real estate signs littered the entrance, advertising lots and waterfront homes for sale.

People barbecued nearby, their lives moving on.

But as I approached the house, there it was: piles of rubble, dumpsters.

The house was gone.

Beyond the "No Trespassing" sign, the land was overgrown. It was greener—but only because it had been left unattended.

Trees and blackened trunks clawed at the sky, a stark silhouette against the daylight. Phantosmia maybe, but the acrid smell of the fire came rushing back.

I stepped closer.

I wasn't searching for objects—I was searching for the piece of myself I had left behind. It's strange how standing among what's left behind sharpens the whole picture, how clarity waits until you're face-to-face with what's no longer there.

Just like that plot of land, I thrived without him.

I toasted with Masie and Maggie at a brunch at The Beverly Hills Hotel on the day *Heavy Metal Headbang* was released, my brain injury story becoming a guide for others navigating their own struggles. Before leaving Pittsburgh, Hilary and Blondie flew in to celebrate my fortieth birthday. Lacey and I caught Aerosmith on their very last tour before they retired for good. I even stood front row at a Judas Priest concert.

My career flourished too, taking me places I'd only dreamed of. I was invited to the legendary Lair of the Hollywood Vampires and was offered a permanent guest list spot at the Whiskey a Go Go. I worked with renowned writers and childhood heroes on projects. I stepped through doors I'd never imagined possible.

At the time, I couldn't see it. I was too sad, too close, tangled up in what had been, weighed down by doubt and hollow exhaustion my ex filled me with and then left behind. But I kept moving, despite being so still mentally in my emotional cul-de-sac, managing inspiration in my darkest hour.

I really had it all.

What I've always wanted.

I worked through it and for it.

Life isn't about finding yourself, it's about creating yourself—over and over.

I came to, turning to get back in my Bronco. "Goddamn," I whispered. Tears brimmed and fell to the dirt. I wasn't sad about all I'd been through or the things I'd lost. I was proud. Proud that I'd come out more badass than ever.

Thank you, wildfire.

Destruction is just as much a beginning as it is an ending.

SEAWEED

THE 2024 ELECTION was a fail. Pluto ended its sixteen-year journey through Capricorn, ushering in the Age of Aquarius. As if reflecting the upheaval of celestial and earthly cycles, a bomb cyclone loomed over the Pacific Northwest. Despite the storm in this strange new chapter, I decided to take a train to Seattle, driven by a series of coincidences I couldn't ignore...

The New York Times announced that Sub Pop Records would remaster and re-release The Gits' catalog for the first time in thirty years, with legendary grunge sound engineer Jack Endino at the helm. The news came just four months after the band's drummer, Steve Moriarty, published his biography, *Mia Zapata & The Gits*. Unaware of any of this, I emailed musician and Home Alive co-founder Gretta Harley earlier in the week. Harley, celebrated for her bands Maxi Badd and Danger Gens, was recognized as one of *Seattle Weekly*'s "50 Women Who Rock Seattle." She also co-wrote and produced *These Streets*, a live music play honoring Seattle's grunge-era female musicians. I'd reached out to her for a book blurb.

A couple of days later, Seattle radio station KEXP announced the live debut of their *Sound & Vision* podcast, featuring Gits members, bassist Matt Dresdner and guitarist Andy Kessler, as guests.

The timing felt personal and serendipitous.

I bought tickets without hesitation, though logistics gave me pause—I had copy edits to finish, a manuscript due, and no clear ending in sight. I was caught in the liminal space between closing one chapter and starting another.

Must was the mantra.

The night before leaving Portland for Seattle, I gave my hair a bleach bath and slathered on toner, dyed my eyebrows and lashes black—a ritual for leaving town. I completed the transformation the next morning with my best ripped vintage 501s, a white Hanes tee, and a necklace strung with a guitar pick that had fallen from Andy Wood's mausoleum, a talisman that felt like carrying a secret strength. I packed an ornamental flannel in my olive duffel—just in case. With my kid's Carhartt jacket slung over my shoulders and my backpack holding a heavy laptop, I felt determined.

The crisp air hitting—it was unmistakably November.

Crossing the bridge to Union Station, the Willamette River lay still, its glassy surface reflecting the skyline.

I braced for a city that still echoed with sounds I couldn't let go of. For as many times as I'd traveled there, the surge of excitement remained.

When I arrived at King Street Station, the south end of Downtown Seattle, I'd just missed the rain. I sat down at Central Tavern, where I spent four hours editing over two snifters of warmed bourbon, surrounded by walls layered with concert flyers—silent relics of a scene that once roared. The empty stage before me felt anything but vacant, its atoms humming with the ghosts of every band I'd ever loved. Most of them are gone now, but their presence lingered, haunting and proud of it.

At Hotel Max, I was greeted by Charles Peterson's iconic black-and-white photography set against a backdrop of deep red walls, each image a shrine to the raw, unfiltered energy of the grunge era.

I'd walked the length of 1st Avenue, from King Street Station to Seattle Center, retracing steps etched into the city's soul. The marine layer clung like a damp veil, softening the skyline scattered with cranes towering like sentinels of change. Among them, relics of the city's past—like the neon Elephant Car Wash sign, defiantly glowing in its rude '50s palette. I couldn't help but think of it as a sarcastic nod from Amazon corporate, a relic preserved to mock nostalgia while its empire devoured everything around it.

When I think of Seattle, it's not the sleek skyscrapers or the streams of backpack-hauling commuters spilling down Pill Hill or Olive Way into the city's core. It's corner-ridden greasy diners with burnt coffee and gritty clubs that once shook the city with amplifier feedback—though few of the original haunts remain. It's the soul lingering in worn edges, clinging to the cracks even as modernity threatens to erase it.

Passing The 5 Point Cafe, nestled near The Space Needle, I thought of the members of Mother Love Bone. That was their place, and you could feel the presence in the booths and greasy counters. I always wondered which side they preferred, what they drank, and if they liked pull tab gambling.

I walked past the Chris Cornell bronze statue at the tip of Seattle Center, through a sprawling Christmas market strung with twinkle lights and carousel music.

There was the International Fountain, where fans leaped in at the end of Kurt Cobain's public vigil in 1994.

Up the stairs past The Vera Project, towards KEXP, where just to the right of the lobby hung a large, neon-painted portrait of Mia Zapata.

Inside, I grabbed a Diet Coke and settled into a chair near the front. Clad in my grunge garb, I felt self-conscious. It wasn't an homage; it was my uniform. But in that moment, it felt like a parody of a past I couldn't bring myself to let go of. Dusky and out of place, I sat among people bundled in North Face puffer vests, their practicality contrasting with my nostalgia.

When Gits members Matt Dresdner and Andy Kessler stepped onto the stage, the room fell silent. This was about Mia—celebrating her life and her gifts.

They shared vivid stories: the time she insulted David Bowie at a gas station after he mistook her for an attendant; her humor and poetic wit. They joked about her go-to response when asked about her lyrics: "The Torment."

Andy shared that one of his favorite songs was "Seaweed," which also happened to be mine. It was mentioned that before her death, the band had been working on an album, but Mia still needed to rework the vocals—leaving some of The Gits songs forever unfinished. I later learned it was because her vocal cords had been damaged by her struggles with drinking and the screaming matches from a recent breakup.

In Steve Moriarty's book, the foreword described the band's music as a universal language—a force that unites, inspires, and heals. Testimonies within its pages told of lives changed by The Gits: a man reconsidered suicide after hearing "Second Skin," a woman escaped abuse with "Social Love," and a cancer survivor drew strength from "Whirlwind."

The Gits weren't just a band—they were a lifeline.

Mia's voice was a testament to the power of turning pain into something beautiful.

Her lyrics reminded me that it was okay to fight and urged me to keep going.

Though their career was tragically cut short, their music remains timeless, a beacon of hope and healing for anyone who needs it—just as I needed them to pull me through the fire, and everything that came after.

It felt like the world was finally catching up to what so many already knew: the band's legacy isn't just about music—it's survival, strength, and a voice that refuses to be silenced.

Inspired and restless, I returned to the hotel, my thoughts racing well into the early morning hours before I finally pulled myself out of bed.

I put on my coat and headed outside. The wind bit as I wandered down the street, through the eerily still Pike Place Market. The iconic market sign glowed dimly against the overcast sky, a beacon that had drawn me in so many years ago. The cobblestones gleamed and the faint briny scent of the Puget Sound hung in the air.

I thought of *Mad Love*, the 1995 film with Drew Barrymore and the band 7 Year Bitch, where that very spot played a supporting role. That movie, along with Doug Pray's *Hype!* documentary had painted Seattle as a place I had to see for myself. Those films were my first glimpse into the world of grunge, devoured on VHS tapes rented from a corner store in the middle of nowhere near my parents' house.

On the bottom floor of the market, a dusty glass case refracted a faint reflection as I passed, reminding me of my eighteen-year-old self who once stood there.

With high school graduation money, I flew to Seattle for the first time. I thought of the green scrapbook I'd lost in the fire, filled with relics from that trip: photos of Sub Pop headquarters, concert flyers, bus tickets, stickers, and scraps of paper. One page had a photo of me in a navy baby tee and brown Dickies, lying on a grassy knoll. Another featured a shot of my first tattoo—the Kill Rock Stars logo freshly etched into my arm. Each piece was proof that I'd been there, that I'd touched something real. Losing that album felt like losing a piece of that experience, but the memories called back to me.

The market was hushed, its labyrinthine layer of floors quieter than I remembered—the absence of crowds made the place feel like it was holding its breath.

Seattle had been more than a city back then—it was a dream made tangible. For a kid who grew up idolizing that world, that scene, walking those streets felt like stepping into the center of the universe. The city still carried its weight, its pull. It had been a refuge for a teenager chasing something they couldn't name, and though time had stripped away much of what was, the heart of what had drawn me here remained.

Outside, the waterfront drew out into the distance, a hazy merging of the sky and sea.

I navigated the streets lost in thought, tracing the incline up Pike to Capitol Hill, and met up with my longtime friend, Joel, at The Comet Tavern, where dim Christmas lights strung haphazardly and an Alice in Chains knock-off humming faintly in the background.

Joel and I both changed since we first met back in Columbus in 2005, where, at a dance club, I insulted his shoes. That was Joel—patient enough to weather my sharp tongue, quick to laugh at the absurdity of it. I'd known Joel to be quietly observant, with a thoughtful gaze surrounded by wire-rimmed glasses. His salt-and-pepper beard, somewhat wiry and unkempt, hinted at a quiet, yet sardonic, and nerdy wisdom. He had become the constant in my life, proof that some connections endure even when everything else seems to burn away. He moved to Seattle with Mika—I'd introduced them back in Portland. They got married, built a life here, and became more like family.

Sitting there with Joel, sharing a table with a bourbon for me, a stout for him, and a vegan BLT that had me side-eyeing his judgment, it felt like nothing had changed at all.

Joel picked up his pint of stout, watching me with that familiar mix of teasing and insight. "How was the KEXP event?" he asked, leaning back.

I smiled. "Incredible."

Joel nodded knowingly, his grin fading into something more thoughtful. "Yeah, I figured it would be. I mean, that's heavy stuff, but exciting."

"It hit hard," I admitted. "Being in that room, hearing them talk about Mia, the band, and everything... it just felt so real. It humanized her. She was *here*. She walked *these streets*, sat in *this bar*."

Joel glanced around, his expression softening. "The Comet," he said quietly. "Last place she was seen alive, right?"

"Yeah," I said, my voice trailed. "You can feel it in here, can't you?"

Joel nodded slowly, his stout untouched in front of him. "That's Seattle."

I smiled, absentmindedly plucking a rogue hair I found on my chin.

Joel continued, "You always wanted to bask in Seattle's grunge scene without fully diving in. It was over though, and living here was too much for you—too big, too expensive, too overwhelming."

I raised a brow and asked, "Is *that* why we moved to Portland?"

Joel leaned back, crossing his arms. "Of course. Portland's three hours away—close enough for you to visit Seattle whenever you wanted, but far enough to keep your cozy bubble intact—being a small-town girl and all."

"Come on!" I protested, laughing. "I got into school in Portland. *That's why*."

"Sure, school was the excuse," he said, waving a hand. "But let's be real—you wanted Seattle close, not in your face. Portland let you flirt without committing."

I groaned. "You make it sound so calculated."

"Wasn't it?" he said with a grin. "And it worked. You got what you wanted without freaking out."

I leaned back, staring down at my bourbon. "Maybe. But it feels different now. I've spent the last two days walking around Seattle, and it's like... I don't need to keep it at arm's length anymore. It feels like I'm finally part of all of it in some weird way."

Joel studied me for a moment, his teasing grin fading into something quieter. "It's a big part of you—and you might be the last person that gives a shit about it," he said, his voice dry but not condescending, almost laughing, in fact.

I was caught off guard by how direct he was. That was Joel—silently sentimental, rarely too forward with his emotions, but when he did let something slip, it stuck.

"And I've been trying to finish the book," I said after a pause.

He tilted his glass with a faint smile. "Ahh, *the book*. You're always writing your way through stuff."

"Yeah, well," I said, my laugh trailing, "it's less wrestling with ghosts and more staring at a blinking cursor, convincing myself I don't totally suck."

Joel shook his head. "That's your problem. You think too much. You've been carrying on about this book for how long? Wandering about for how long? Maybe Seattle's exactly where you're supposed to crack it open and let it out."

"You just broke the fourth wall," I said.

"Maybe," he said. "Or maybe you just needed someone to tell you what you already knew."

He stopped mid-thought to swat at a gnat, shaking his head. "There was this fruit fly in my house that's been driving me insane for days. Pretty sure it came in with some bananas. I'd been trying not to kill it. You know I'm not religious, and I'm definitely not Buddhist, but I made this whole decision to stop killing bugs unless I absolutely have to. Except mosquitoes—those I can't stand—Anyway, last night I was sitting there watching TV, and I felt something on my forehead. Instinct kicked in—I smacked it without thinking. Killed it. After all that effort to let it live. You can put that in your book."

I almost choked on my bourbon. "Oh, I will!"

The Comet suddenly felt different, like a symbol of everything I'd let go of and everything I'd reclaimed. It wasn't just about being in Seattle or returning to Portland—it was about being back in the Pacific Northwest, surrounded by my friends, finally stable for the first time in years.

The music carried me, stitching together the pieces I feared I'd lost.

I realized I wasn't running anymore.

I didn't need to save myself.

Not from anything. Not from anyone. Not anymore.

If you or anyone you know is a victim of domestic abuse please contact:

US The National Domestic Violence Hotline:
1-800-799-SAFE
or visit https://www.thehotline.org/

UK National Domestic Abuse helpline: 0808 2000 247
or visit https://www.nationaldahelpline.org.uk/

Respect (for men experiencing domestic abuse):
0808 8010 327 or visit https://mensadviceline.org.uk/

Australia 1800RESPECT: 1800 737 732
or visit https://1800respect.org.au/

ACKNOWLEDGMENTS

TO ALL OF my friends—thank you for standing by me through the moments that shaped this story. This journey is my own, but I am deeply grateful for the love, support, and approval you offered as I shared pieces of it with the world.

I navigated the aftermath of life's challenges, and it was your friendship that reminded me of the strength in connection and the power of resilience. Thank you from the bottom of my heart.

ABOUT THE AUTHOR

BORN AND RAISED in rural Pennsylvania, Melissa Meszaros has set the precedent for breaking tropes and forging the way for the modern nomadic. As a tenured entertainment industry publicist, Melissa is also the founder of Grrrl Front PDX Music Festival and the comic book publicity firm, Don't Hide PR. She is a self-proclaimed grunge aficionado, graduate of Antioch University Los Angeles' MFA in Creative Writing, and proudly shares a birthday with Melvins leader, Buzz Osborne.

Her previous book, *Heavy Metal Headbang* is also available from Oil On Water Press.

Oil On Water Press
Original true-life stories and memoir

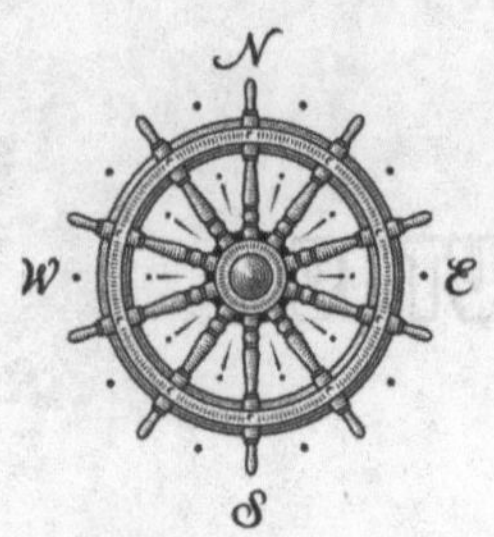

THE TOWN SLOWLY EMPTIES: On Life and Culture during Lockdown by Manash Firaq Bhattacharjee A latter-day Journal of the Plague Year. The author rekindles ties with culture, and affirms friendship, empathy and love.

SMALL TOWN SKATEPARKS by Clint Carrick A skateboarding road trip celebrating the institution of the skatepark in America's small towns.

A BROOKLYN MEMOIR: My Life as a Boy by Robert Rosen Brooklyn, 1955–64: A Jewish boy learns about life and death from the W.W. II vets and Holocaust survivors who surround him.

HEAVY METAL HEADBANG by Melissa Meszaros After being hit by a car on the way to a Judas Priest concert, Melissa Meszaros' life is turned upside down by a traumatic brain injury.

LETTING GO THE LEASH by Stephen Ellis Hamilton Redemptive tale set against a tornado and a pandemic. Banker Stephen Ellis Hamilton quits his job of thirty-four years to save a rescue dog. And himself.

A WAY UP: 1 Woman Across the Pacific NW by Paula Engborg An energetic, 41-year-old divorcee in search of Prince Charming one day finds a new sport. Paula Engborg has barely ascended a stepladder, so why the desire to climb mountains?

WALK THIS WAY by Duncan McNamara Duncan McNamara sets off with a rucksack of mostly useless items on a 500-mile from the French foothills of the Pyrenees to the Shrine of St James the Great.

THE HEART IS MEAT An 80s Memoir New York City's Meatpacking District in the 1980s. An incredible true story.

www.ingramcontent.com/pod-product-compliance
Lightning Source LLC
LaVergne TN
LVHW040727021025
822365LV00006B/11

9781915316479